EFFECTIVE EARLY LEARNING
Case Studies in Improvement

CHRISTINE PASCAL & TONY BERTRAM

SERIES EDITOR TINA BRUCE

Effective Early Learning Research Project

P·C·P
Paul Chapman
Publishing

DEDICATION

This book is dedicated to all those children who we hope have felt the impact of effective early learning.

ACKNOWLEDGMENTS

We would like to thank all the practitioners, parents and children who have worked together with us to develop the Effective Early Learning process.
We are very grateful for the financial support provided by the Esmée Fairbairn Charitable Trust and the Baring Foundation.

Reprinted 2001

Paul Chapman Publishing Ltd
A SAGE Publications Company
6 Bonhill Street
London EC2A 4PU

SAGE Publications Inc
2455 Teller Road
Thousand Oaks, California 91320

SAGE Publications India Pvt Ltd
32, M-Block Market
Greater Kailash - I
New Delhi 110 048

British Library Cataloguing in Publication data
A catalogue record for this book is available from the British Library

ISBN   0 7619 7293 5

Library of Congress catalog card number

Reprinted for SAGE publications by Alden Press

First published 1997
Impression number   10   9   8   7   6   5   4   3   2   1
Year   2000   1999   1998   1997

Copyright © 1997 Christine Pascal and Tony Bertram

CONTENTS

Series Preface – 0–8 years   v

Introduction   1
    Christine Pascal and Tony Bertram

1: Case Study One – An LEA Nursery School   18
    Jan Georgeson

2: Case Study Two – A Family Centre   32
    Tina Bruce, Margy Whalley, Katie Mairs, Cath Arnold, and the
    Centre team

3: Case Study Three – A Private Day Nursery   52
    Janet Dye

4: Case Study Four – A Preschool Playgroup   66
    Fiona Ramsden

5: Case Study Five – A Social Services Day Nursery   83
    Maureen Saunders

6: Case Study Six – A Nursery Class within a Primary School   98
    Janet Dye

7: Case Study Seven – A Private Day Nursery   111
    Fiona Ramsden

8: Case Study Eight – A Workplace Nursery   128
    Sarah Kelly

9: Case Study Nine – A Primary School Reception Class   138
    Tony Bertram

10: Reflections and Emerging Issues   150
    Christine Pascal and Tony Bertram

Bibliography   160

Index   167

Series Preface – 0–8 Years

At most times in history and in most parts of the world, the first eight years of life have been seen as the first phase of living. Ideally, during this period, children learn who they are; about those who are significant to them; and how their world is. They learn to take part, and how to contribute creatively, imaginatively, sensitively and reflectively.

Children learn through and with the people they love, and the people who care for them. They learn through being physically active, through real, direct experiences, and through learning how to use and make symbolic systems, such as play, language and representation.

Whether children are at home, in nursery schools, classes, family centres, day nurseries, playgroups (now re-named preschools), workplace nurseries or primary schools, they need informed adults who can help them.

The 0–8 series will help those who work with young children, in whatever capacity, to be as informed as possible about this first phase of living.

From the age of 8 years old, the developing and learning can be consolidated, hopefully in ways which build on what has gone before.

In this series, each book emphasises a different aspect of the first stage of living (0–8 years).

Getting To Know You: A Guide to Record Keeping in Early Childhood Education and Care by Lynne Bartholomew and Tina Bruce is based on principles of good practice in the spirit of Stephen Isaacs. It explores the relationship between observation, assessment, evaluation and monitoring in a record keeping system. It takes account of legal requirements in the different parts of the UK. The book is full of examples of good practice in record keeping. Unless we know and understand our children, unless we act effectively on what we know, we cannot help them very much.

Learning to be Strong: Integrating Education and Care in Early Childhood by Margy Whalley is an inspirational book. Pen Green Centre for Under-fives and their Families in Corby, Northamptonshire, is an acknowledged beacon of excellence, emulated throughout the UK and internationally. When adults come together as a team – parents, educators, carers, those in Social Services and Health experts using their energy on behalf of the child – then education and care become truly integrated. Just as it was important that Margaret McMillan's pioneer work at the turn of the century in integrating education and care should be recorded, so this book has become a classic of the 1990s.

Beacons of excellence, like Pen Green, when documented in this way, can continue to illuminate principles which influence quality practice through the ages, transcending the passing of time.

Helping Children to Draw and Paint in Early Childhood: Children and Visual Representation by John Matthews gives a fascinating insight into the early drawings, paintings and models that children make. The book shows how these begin and traces development from scribbles to later drawings in the period of the first eight years. A wealth of real life examples is given, together with practical strategies that adults can use to help children develop their drawings and paintings with quality.

In *Helping Children to Learn through a Movement Perspective*, Mollie Davies, an internationally respected movement expert with years of practical experience of working with young children, writes about the central places of movement within the learning process. In a lively, well-illustrated book, with lots of real examples, she makes a case for movement as a common denominator of the total development of children, and in this draws our attention to its integrating function. A whole chapter is devoted to dance – the art form of movement. The provision of a readily accessible movement framework gives excellent opportunities for adults to plan, observe and record their children's development in movement terms.

Self-Esteem and Successful Early Learning by Rosemary Roberts is about the importance of being positive, encouraging and gently firm in bringing up and working with young children. Whilst every family is different, every family shares some aspects of living with young children. These are taken up and given focus in the book in ways that are accessible and lead to practical strategies. The reader meets a variety of situations with the family and explores successful ways of tackling them so that the theories supporting the practice become meaningful and useful.

The Development of Language and Literacy by Marion Whitehead emphasises the importance of adults being sensitive to the child's culture, feeling and ideas as language develops and early attempts to communicate in writing and reading emerge. Bilingualism and its indications are looked at in depth. Children need to spend time with people who care about them, enjoy being with them, and sensitively support their early language and literacy.

Resources for Early Learning: Children, Adults and Stuff by Pat Gura takes a critical look at the materials that are given to children in early years settings and examines the conventional wisdom and assumptions that early years workers make about resources such as sand, water, paint, blocks, the home area and others. The book encourages practitioners to be reflective.

Effective Early Learning edited by Christine Pascal and Tony Bertram is about practitioner research. It shows how nine very different early childhood settings experienced the Effective Early Learning project. This research project is about empowering practitioners to develop their own practice and is having a great influence and impact on the quality of practice in the UK.

Clinging to dogma, 'I believe children need . . .' or saying 'What was good enough for me . . .' is not good enough. Children deserve better than that. The pursuit of excellence means being informed. This series will help adults to increase their knowledge and understanding of the 'first phase of living', and to act in the light of this for the good of children.

TINA BRUCE

INTRODUCTION

Christine Pascal and Tony Bertram

THE EFFECTIVE EARLY LEARNING PROJECT

This book contains a selection of nine case studies from the group of early childhood settings in the first phase of a research project entitled Effective Early Learning: An Action Plan for Change (the EEL Project). The first phase of the EEL Project was a purely developmental one, during which practitioners, parents and children from these settings worked closely with a group of researchers based at Worcester College of Higher Education. The aim of this first stage of work was to create a methodology for evaluating and developing the quality of early learning in a diverse range of education and care settings for 3 and 4 year olds in the UK. The methodology developed in this first phase was further consolidated, trialled, developed and extended beyond the original age limits in subsequent phases of the Project and a substantive base of research evidence was gathered. The analysis of this EEL research data will form the basis of future publications and does not form the material for this book. This book is aimed primarily at practitioners and is intended to provide a first-hand and practical account of the benefits and impact such collaborative partnerships can have on improving the quality of practice. Given the philosophical and professional focus of this Project, symbolically this seemed to be the right place to start. More publications will follow, aimed at similar and different audiences, but all will have the same expressed aim of improving the quality of educational provision for young children.

Background to the Project

In this Introduction the context and evolution of the EEL Project is described and its theoretical and philosophical underpinnings are made explicit. The EEL approach to quality improvement, and the EEL evaluative framework and methodology are also outlined. This provides the reader with an understanding of the scope and breadth of the evaluative process that was undertaken by the participants in the Project. The nine case studies which follow share a common aim of improving the quality of their provision. These case studies are drawn from a wide range of education and care settings. They represent the state, voluntary and private sectors, and deliberately straddle the education and care divide. It is hoped that these case studies provide authentic examples of a dynamic, developmental and collaborative process, which led to real improvements in practice and provision. The individual nature of each case study emphasises the fact that there is no magic wand for improving quality. The transformation must come from within and is achieved through the mobilisation and development of the expertise and experience of those who work with the children. What is needed is a framework and a set of support mechanisms to get the process underway. All the case study settings went through a similar evaluative process but each one did so in its own way. The improvements which flowed from the Action Plans were many and varied, reflecting individual circumstances and needs. What this diversity of response illustrates is the need for flexibility within a coherent evaluative framework. The case studies may be useful in a number of ways:

- exploring ways of working in collaborative partnerships;

- as examples of developmental planning for various aspects of practice;

- for in-depth experiences of an improvement process which aims to empower and strengthen those who undertake it;

- in staff development sessions which focus on the management of change;

- to review the issues surrounding evaluation and improvement in early childhood settings;

- for staff preparation before an evaluation or inspection process.

The final chapter in this book looks across the experience of these first-phase case studies and draws out some of the issues which need to be considered by those who are committed to a process of validated self-evaluation and improvement.

The EEL Project began work in May 1993 and grew out of the urgent need for procedures to facilitate quality evaluation and improvement in the diverse range of settings in which under-5s are being educated in the UK. It also responded to the lack of a substantial empirical database on the quality and effectiveness of early learning offered in these settings. It focuses particularly on provision for 3 and 4 year olds, as these children are currently in a wider range of provision than any other age group, but its methods and principles are applicable to teaching and learning at any age. The Project is operating throughout the UK and is being carried out by a team of practitioner researchers, directed by Professor Christine Pascal and Dr Tony Bertram, based at the Centre for Research in Early Childhood at Worcester College of Higher Education in the UK.

The aims of the Project

The key aims of the Project are:

1   To develop a cost-effective strategy to evaluate and improve the quality and effectiveness of early learning available to 3 and 4 year old children in a wide range of education and care settings across England, Wales, Scotland and Northern Ireland.
2   To evaluate and compare rigorously and systematically the quality of early learning provided in the diverse range of early childhood education and care settings which characterise provision in the UK.

A strategy for change and improvement

The Project provides a clear and targeted strategy for change and improvement, which builds upon the existing range of provision for young children and attempts to extend the skills and expertise of all those who work with young children. It brings together education and care provision, and includes those in the voluntary, public and private sectors. It centres round the development and application of an innovative, cost-effective and manageable set of Quality Evaluation and Improvement procedures which may be used for training, institutional development, monitoring and review in all early childhood settings. The development of quantitative and qualitative instruments to evaluate and compare the quality of provision in different settings is also a key feature of the Project. In short, it has developed, trialled extensively, and disseminated, a manageable and practicable system of 'externally validated evaluation and improvement' which may be used in all centre-based provision for young children with an educational commitment.

The Project has at its heart two interlinked and complementary elements: research and development. A main thrust of the Project's work is to develop and improve the quality and effectiveness of young children's learning. This operates through the implementation of a process of externally validated self-evaluation, which leads directly to action planning and improvement. It is this aspect of the Project which is the focus of this book.

Development of the Project

The Effective Early Learning Project has evolved through a number of phases. In the first three phases:

- 700+ settings have undertaken the quality evaluation and improvement process

- 3,000+ practitioners and external advisers have been trained in the EEL procedures

- 20,000+ children and their families have benefited from the process.

The Project has been, and continues to be, developmental and collaborative. From the onset, we worked in partnership with practitioners, and during the last four years this partnership has grown and evolved. In particular, the practitioners in later phases of the project have taken over responsibility for most of the evaluation and improvement process, benefiting from the support and validation of an EEL External Adviser at key points. This 'groundedness' provides the EEL procedures with validity, credibility and strength. The experience of the last four years have shown that Quality Evaluation and Improvement is a process well within the grasp of all those who work with young children. Those we have worked with have embraced the rigorous and critical procedures with professionalism and dedication, and an overriding commitment to improving the quality of their work with young children.

The nine case studies which are presented in this book are all drawn from the first phase of the Project, when the EEL Support Workers in each setting were all members of the central team, exploring how far practitioners were able, and prepared, to take on the procedures themselves. Their contributions to the assessment of the process were invaluable in its development and, in particular, in ensuring it was relevant, manageable and accessible. Following their feedback, in subsequent phases, the practitioners have been trained to take on this role, with the support of an EEL External Adviser. In this way the Project has become more democratic and rigorous as time has gone on.

The Project and how young children learn

We have never known so much about how young children learn and how this learning may be most effectively supported by the adults surrounding young children. The EEL Project builds on this extensive research evidence and aims to help practitioners incorporate this knowledge into their professional practice. The Project has a number of theoretical sources for its work on learning and teaching, which have been further validated and extended by more recent research and development in the field. In the Project we focus clearly on:

- the quality of the educative relationship between child and adult;

- helping practitioners to look at the learning/teaching process in a critical reflective and informed way.

Whilst acknowledging the enormous contribution of Piaget (1968, 1986) to our understanding of children's development and schematic understanding of the world, the Project draws fundamentally upon Vygotsky's (1978) work on the importance of the social context of children's learning.

Vygotsky's work

Vygotsky's work demonstrated that children's learning is a social activity which progresses through interaction with adults and other children. He proposed that at any one time children's learning has three levels or 'zones' of development:

- The Zone of Actual Development (ZAD)

- The Zone of Proximal Development (ZPD)

- The Zone of Future Development (ZFD).

Vygotsky's Zone of Actual Development describes the learning the child has already mastered. The Zone of Future Development describes the learning that the child has yet to experience and grasp. However, the key to effective learning is the Zone of Proximal Development. This is the area of learning where the child is challenged: she has the learning within her grasp but has not yet achieved competency. The child is required to operate at the edge of her capabilities. It demands that the child moves forward her current state of knowledge, understanding and abilities. Often this is also where the child needs an adult or peer, who can support her as she reaches forward developmentally into new learning and beyond her existing level of competency. Effective educators strive to ensure the child encounters such challenges in a positive way and meets opportunities to extend herself, at least some of the time. Educators who operate in the ZAD are merely reinforcing what is already learnt. Rehearsing prior knowledge can substantially be left to the child. Educators who operate in the ZFD will find it difficult to attach new knowledge to a child's current understanding. The ZPD is the area where knowledge is extended most effectively in a supported expansion of understanding.

Effective educators are able to recognise children operating in this Zone, and step in to support and extend the learning when this is appropriate. The ability to recognise this Zone is very important to those who wish to work effectively with young children.

The contribution of Csikszentmihayli (1992) can help. He argued that, when children's skills and capabilities are appropriately matched and challenged, children can be seen to be in what he termed 'a State of Flow'. Here physical and mental activity are in harmony, working creatively within the child to lead her forward developmentally and intellectually.

Involvement

Laevers (1993, 1996) has taken this concept further and identifies what he terms the state of 'Involvement'. He describes children who are operating at the 'edge of their capabilities' and in a 'state of flow' as being at a high level of Involvement. This term is used to describe a particular quality of human activity and not just used to refer to the state of 'busy-ness' of the child. An involved child is totally focused, concentrating intently and immersed in the activity she is doing, be it social, mathematical, linguistic, scientific, spiritual or, more probably, all of these. Laevers (1993) defines the concept of Involvement as:

a quality of human activity, characterised by concentration and persistence, a high level of motivation, intense perceptions and experiencing of meaning, a strong flow of energy, a high degree of satisfaction, and based on the exploratory drive and basic development of schemes.   (p. 61)

He argues that children who achieve this state of Involvement are using a great deal of mental energy in order to respond to their exploratory drive, and that this kind of mental activity leads to shifts in the child's fundamental schemata. His work suggests that over time this level of experience leads to the child being able to operate at a higher level. In short, deep level learning occurs within the child and this may be demonstrated by enhanced performance on measures of learning outcome. The EEL Project is also collecting evidence of this process in action. Research on motivation from the United States also shows that children who are motivated, enthusiastic, able to persist, concentrate and focus their energies (demonstrating Involvement) perform better on outcome measures of performance (Brown and Palinscar, 1989).

This work also stresses the importance of providing children with a measure of control over the learning process and opportunities to self-manage and organise if these qualities or dispositions are to be mobilised within the child. In addition, work by Dweck and her colleagues (Dweck and Elliot 1979), on children with a 'mastery orientation' to learning has shown the significance of these dispositions to later educational achievement.

THE EEL PROJECT AND QUALITY PROVISION

The EEL Project is based on the belief that 'quality' is a value-laden, subjective and dynamic concept which varies with time, perspective and place (Pascal and Bertram et al. 1996). This belief has grown out of our experience which has shown that to lay down precise, fixed, static definitions of quality is inappropriate. Rather, we have found that evaluation is more powerful, accurate and valid if it grows out of the shared and agreed perspective of those who are closest to the experiences being assessed.

However, we were also mindful that there are aspects of practice and provision which provide a core set of conditions which favour high quality early learning experiences. There is a wide consensus amongst theorists and practitioners about the essentials of quality in early childhood provision and our experience in working with some 3,000 practitioners from all over the UK during the Project has confirmed this.

An evaluative framework

Although we embrace an approach to defining quality which is dynamic, developmental and allows for differing value bases, it was also clear to us that to be successful, an evaluation project needed to employ a clear and systematic framework. The EEL Project, therefore, working with practitioners, managers, parents and children, developed a framework for evaluating quality which builds upon the consensus about what constitutes quality in early childhood and also the knowledge base we have about effective early learning. This evaluative framework is represented diagrammatically on page 8.

This framework is flexible, and allows for individual interpretation, but is formed around a number of clear 'domains' or 'dimensions' of quality practice which allows for comparability and cohesiveness within the Project as a whole. The framework employed in the EEL Project (Pascal and Bertram 1994a, b, Pascal et al. 1995, Pascal et al. 1996) may be taken as a typical example of many other evaluative frameworks for early childhood within the UK and demonstrates the breadth of issues that any evaluation of quality must embrace.

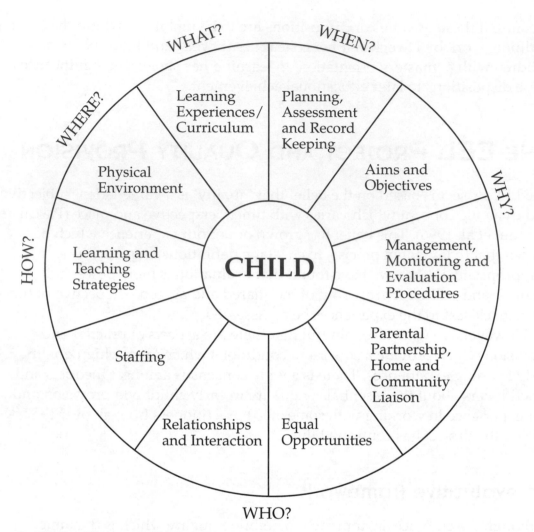

Figure 1   The Pascal/Bertram Quality Evaluation Framework

The framework has the following 10 dimensions:

- Aims and Objectives.

- Learning Experiences/Curriculum.

- Learning and Teaching Strategies.

- Planning, Assessment and Record Keeping.

- Staffing.

- Physical Environment.

- Relationships and Interactions.

- Equal Opportunities.

- Parental Partnership, Home and Community Liaison.

- Management, Monitoring and Evaluation.

Values and principles

The recent priority accorded to developing quality across the diversity of early childhood settings in the UK has spawned a growing number of initiatives. Some of these have a clear focus on measuring or assessing quality as part of a policy for quality inspection or assurance. Other initiatives are geared towards quality improvement or total quality management, developed as part of a provider's commitment towards raising standards. A useful topology and critique of these various approaches can be found in Williams' evaluation of approaches to quality in early childhood services (Williams 1995). All of these schemes build upon the established consensus of the key elements of quality provision (DES 1990, DoH 1991), and each has an expressed commitment to raising standards in early childhood provision.

The literature provides much reassurance that improvement need not be a threatening process but can be achieved in a positive, empowering way. We have found substantial agreement as to the strategies which appear to facilitate effective quality improvement and those which do not. These common strategies reveal the following.

- Judgements about quality need to be made.

- An outside perspective is required and that the assessed and the assessor know and trust each other.

- Evaluation should emerge from an open, honest and collaborative dialogue using a shared vocabulary.

- This dialogue should be generated over an extended period of time.

- The dialogue should have a clear, systematic and agreed framework and format.

- The evidence for evaluation is gathered together and shared together.

- The evaluation process should lead to action plans.

- The action should be followed through, supported and monitored.

- The settings should take ownership of the process and its outcomes.

- All participants in the process should be encouraged to make a contribution which is acknowledged and valued.

- Compulsion and hierarchies do not work. Collaboration and participation do work.

We believe these common characteristics of effective quality improvement provide a sound basis from which to plan further action in the field of early childhood.

Approaching evaluation democratically

Another underlying conception in the EEL Project is a 'democratic approach' to quality evaluation (Pfeffer and Coote 1991). As quality evaluation is a value-laden enterprise, we believe it is best achieved through the active involvement of participants in the process. Thus, the evaluation process is viewed as something 'done with' participants and not 'done to' them.

The subjectivity of the definition is thus acknowledged and the shared perceptions of quality are celebrated as central to the debate about quality in each particular setting. Quality is defined by the shared reflections and agreement of experienced practitioners, parents and children. It is validated and scrutinised for accuracy by those closest to the learning experiences being evaluated.

The EEL Project is therefore firmly founded on democratic principles and the team have worked hard to establish a feeling of partnership and shared ownership of the whole research process – although we might discuss at some length the distribution of power within these relationships. Our philosophical commitment to this approach was reinforced with the hope that it would also help the 'Evaluation and Improvement' process become a major vehicle for the professional development of the practitioners. We also hoped that it would ensure that the individual settings would become more responsive, more fit for purpose and that those within them would be empowered by the process (Pfeffer and Coote 1991).

The Evaluation and Improvement Process

Building on the above principles of action, quality is evaluated using the EEL framework by taking the participants through a systematic and rigorous four-stage process of Evaluation and Improvement.

Stage 1: Evaluation. Researchers and participants work together to document and evaluate the quality of early learning within the setting.

Stage 2: Action Planning. Participants meet together to identify priorities for action and to generate an Action Plan to implement this.

Stage 3: Improvement. The Action Plan to improve the quality of provision is implemented.

Stage 4: Reflection. Participants are encouraged to reflect upon the Evaluation and Improvement process and to review the impact of the Action Plan in the light of experience.

1 Evaluation stage

In the first phase of Evaluation, the team of practitioners within the setting work together with an EEL External Adviser, parents and children to scrutinise the quality of their provision. The quality of practice in relation to each of the 10 dimensions of quality is carefully documented and evaluated using a number of research methods in which the Project participants are trained. These include detailed observations of children and adults, interviews of parents, colleagues and children, documentary analysis and a number of questionnaires. One of the key and innovatory features of this Project is that it allows a detailed, rigorous quantitative and qualitative assessment to be made of the quality of educational provision across a wide range of different early childhood settings. This process of quality assessment has been enhanced by the utilisation of two key observation techniques which measure the effectiveness of the learning and teaching processes. These two methods are:

- **the Child Involvement Scale** which measures the level of involvement (deep level learning) of the children in the activities offered

- **the Adult Engagement Scale** which measures the qualities of effective teaching demonstrated by the adult.

The social psychological underpinning of these techniques and their methodology are detailed by Laevers (1996). As these two techniques are so central to the Project's action a short summary of their content and the way we have used them is outlined below.

The Child Involvement Scale is an observation instrument which aims to measure the level of a child's involvement in an activity. We were attracted to it because it is child-focused and it attempts to measure the processes of learning, rather than to concentrate on outcomes. We have also found it to be grounded in a commonsense (and theoretically underpinned) view of effective early learning which all the practitioners in the Project have found accessible and easy to use. It is based on the notion that when children are learning at a 'deep level' (Laevers 1993) they display certain characteristics, which Laevers summarises in the concept of Involvement. This concept is linked directly to children's exploratory drive and also captures the level of concentration and motivation of the child. Laevers argues that the level of involvement a child displays is a key indicator of the quality and effectiveness of that learning experience. Involvement can be seen to be linked to notions of 'match' between ability and the challenge of an activity. Involvement also reflects the purposefulness, relevance and interest of the activity for the child. Involvement levels are deduced from the presence or absence of a number of 'involvement signals' (Laevers 1994) which include:

- concentration

- energy

- creativity

- facial expression and posture

- persistence

- precision

- reaction time

- language

- satisfaction.

Children's involvement can thus be graded on a scale of 1 to 5; level 1 being given when a child displays No Involvement and level 5 being given when a child displays Intense Involvement. Working in conjunction with Laevers, the Worcester team have utilised an English translation of the instrument (Laevers 1996) which has been used successfully within the Project and which we believe has the potential for much wider application.

The Adult Engagement Scale (Laevers 1996, Bertram 1996) provides the second part of the quality assessment process. This instrument is also based on a method developed by Laevers' EXE Project but we have modified it for use in the EEL Project. This evaluative instrument provides an assessment measure of the quality of an adult's interactions with a child. The instrument is based on the notion that the style of interactions between the educator and the child is a critical factor in the effectiveness of the learning experience. The EEL Project identifies three core elements in a teacher's style which shapes the quality of such interactions.

- **Sensitivity.** This is the sensitivity of the adult to the feelings and wellbeing of the child and includes elements of sincerity, empathy, responsiveness and affection.

- **Stimulation.** This is the way in which the adult intervenes in a learning process and the content of such interventions.

- **Autonomy.** This is the degree of freedom which the adult gives the child to experiment, make judgments, choose activities and express ideas. It also includes how the adult handles conflict, rules and behavioural issues.

These two quantitative research methods provide data of the effect of action on the learning and teaching in each setting, as scores obtained in the Evaluation stage can be compared with scores following the Improvement stage. Interestingly, although we term this data 'quantitative' they are both attempts to measure 'qualitative' aspects of the teaching and learning process.

All the qualitative and quantitative data are collated into a detailed and carefully structured Evaluation Report of the quality of early learning within each setting. This Report is fed back to the practitioners in the study setting for validation by the contributors. It is discussed by the participants and carefully evaluated. The perceptions and views of all participants are given status and acknowledgement. Contradictions, agreements, common themes and issues are identified. This stage should take approximately 10 to 12 weeks in total.

2 Action planning stage

Following their evaluation, the practitioners identify priorities for action and, importantly, the resources and expertise required to achieve these. Discussion with managers and other resource holders is essential during this phase and the practitioners must be prepared to promote and explain carefully what is required and why. The practitioners should also explore as many sources of support as possible. Creative and radical approaches to finding the required resources may be needed and the practitioners should not be afraid to try these.

Communicating clearly to all those who will be involved in the Action Plan – what is to happen, how they can help – is a critical part of this phase of the improvement process. Helping people to feel involved, and giving them some ownership and investment in the improvement process, helps to ensure their support, and also shares the burden of any changes which are required.

Children, parents, members of the local community and colleagues all have something to contribute and are offered the opportunity to do so. It is necessary to organise meetings which provide real opportunities for dialogue and sharing. At the end of this stage a structured and realistic Action Plan should emerge which has clearly defined objectives to be achieved within an identified timescale (generally six to nine months). This stage should take approximately two weeks.

3 Improvement stage

In the third stage the Action Plan is implemented. This entails a programme of individual and/or institutional development which relates closely to the agreed priorities. Throughout this stage progress through the Action Plan is monitored and the practitioners are encouraged to gather evidence and reflect upon the effect of the action on the quality of learning in the setting. Again, regular and systematic observation of children and adults is critically important to enable any judgment to be made about the effectiveness of the improvement process. This stage should take approximately six months, but this may be considerably shorter or longer, depending on the extent of the changes proposed.

4 Reflection stage

In this final stage the practitioners are encouraged to reflect upon the Evaluation and Improvement Process, and to review the impact of their Action Plan in the light of experience. It is particularly important that the practitioners look carefully at the effect of the action upon the quality of the children's learning and scrutinise the evidence of this. This process is facilitated by the two assessment instruments (Involvement and Engagement) being carried out again and compared with the previous results to capture any changes in the quality of learning engendered by the Improvement Process. This final stage should take approximately two weeks and should then lead into a further cycle of Evaluation and Improvement.

Throughout this whole process the practitioners are supported by their EEL External Adviser. They also become part of an EEL Local Network consisting of a cluster of participating settings who meet every six weeks to review progress, identify issues, resolve problems and provide practical and moral support. It cannot be denied that implementing this four-stage process is demanding. Experience has shown that the role of the EEL External Adviser and the EEL Local Network are critical to its success. Practitioners who wish to evaluate and improve the quality of learning in their setting need to bear in mind that this process will not be achieved overnight and without effort. Effective and long-term improvement takes time and commitment. We estimate that the whole cycle of Evaluation and Improvement embodied in the EEL Project will take at least 12 months to implement. This timescale may need to be extended if the setting is unaccustomed to this kind of self-evaluation and development process, or if the proposed improvements are fundamental and involve considerable resourcing in both material and human terms. Less fundamental improvements may be achieved in a shorter timescale. Time is a precious commodity in the present climate but the benefits of such a commitment to improvement are wide-ranging and necessary if the issue of learning quality is to be addressed.

Inspection and accreditation

The EEL Evaluative Framework has been developed to dovetail into the various inspection and accreditation frameworks which apply to early childhood settings. The Social Service Inspection Schedule (DoH 1991), the Inspection Framework for LEA Nursery Schools and Classes (OFSTED 1993 and 1996), the Framework for Inspection used in conjunction with the voucher-funded Nursery Education Scheme (DfEE 1996), and the PLA Accreditation Scheme (PPA 1993) all identify certain aspects of the provision which are to be evaluated. These aspects include the physical context, the curriculum and programme, planning and assessment procedures, the quality of teaching or adult interaction and partnerships with parents. Each of these are embraced in the EEL Evaluative Framework and practitioners who progress through Stage 1 of the EEL Process will be collecting systematic evidence about these domains, which may be very useful in preparing for, and responding to, these inspections.

Practitioners who have worked through the EEL Evaluation and Improvement Process have commented that it has been a very valuable and formative experience, providing both a preparation for inspection and a means of moving towards action and improvement following inspection. In a number of cases, the Inspector's Report has specifically cited the impact of the EEL Evaluation and Improvement Process within the nursery, and praised its contribution to the development of practice and the quality of the provision.

THE IMPACT OF THE EEL PROJECT

The EEL Evaluation and Improvement Process has been used by practitioners across the range of different settings which cater for young children. It has worked successfully in the state, voluntary and private sectors and across education and care services. It has proved to be accessible to practitioners with a

TABLE 1: ACTION INITIATIVES UNDERTAKEN IN NINE CASE STUDY SETTINGS

SETTING	Curriculum	Learning and teaching strategies	Planning, assessment and record keeping	Staffing	Physical environment	Relationships and interaction	Equal opportunities	Parental partnership	Management monitoring and evaluation
Reception class	✓				✓				
Social Services day nursery					✓		✓		
LEA nursery class	✓			✓	✓			✓	
Private day nursery	✓			✓					
LEA nursery school	✓			✓				✓	
Pre-school playgroup	✓	✓	✓	✓					
Private day nursery	✓	✓	✓					✓	
Workplace nursery	✓	✓						✓	
Family centre			✓						

range of qualifications, from the relatively untrained to those with higher degrees.

The impact of EEL has been wide-ranging and extensive. In the first phase of operation alone, some 42 action initiatives were generated by the 13 participating early childhood settings. These initiatives covered all aspects of their provision and practice. Some focused on curriculum, others on organisation, outside environment, assessment, staff deployment and teaching style. The two most popular action initiatives were developments in the level of autonomy offered to children and enhancing parental partnerships.

In the nine case studies included in this book there are 28 action initiatives undertaken. These are summarised in Table 1 opposite. A breakdown of these actions show that the EEL Evaluation and Improvement Process is comprehensive and facilitates the identification of a wide range of strengths and weaknesses within a setting. The following chapters describe how the practitioners within the case study settings worked together to arrive at their evaluative conclusions, how they went about addressing their action priorities, the issues they had to tackle in doing so, and how successful they were in achieving their aims. We believe they provide a story of dedication, commitment, hard work and openness to development. They may be used for guidance for those attempting similar changes to their practice, exemplars of the management of change for staff development sessions and real stories of the Improvement Process in action for those about to embark on a similar course. It is hoped that they will be a source of inspiration for those who want to see how developments in practice may be achieved.

1 Case Study One – An LEA Nursery School

Jan Georgeson

Context

This chapter describes the EEL Evaluation and Development Process in an LEA nursery in a metropolitan borough. The nursery was set in extensive gardens on a busy through road and backed on to an infant school and playing fields. The surrounding area was pleasant with large houses and gardens with plenty of trees. Nearby was the tube station and a row of small shops. The nursery had retained much of the character of a large Victorian house with its original layout of rooms, which were shared between three groups of children. The architectural features of the building, such as the fireplaces and stained glass windows, made attractive backdrops to displays. The building lent itself well to division into large and small areas, messy rooms, quiet rooms and cosy corners.

The beautiful garden was one of the setting's biggest assets, offering a range of play equipment and play environments, open spaces and secret dens, with a range of hard and soft (and sometimes 'squishy') surfaces. The trees provided shady areas to escape the heat of the summer sun. The garden was used all year round, with more activities moving outside during the summer months.

There were seven full-time staff at the nursery: a headteacher, three teachers and three nursery nurses. All the teachers had attended courses giving them extra training for working in early years education. There was a part-time secretary and a part-time welfare assistant supporting a child with special educational needs. The nursery provided practical experience for a range of students following PGCE, NNEB, BTEC and sixth form courses.

At the time of the Project there were 146 children attending the nursery, divided equally between 3 and 4 year olds. The children came from families with a wide range of occupations. There was a high proportion of parents engaged in (or with recent experience of) professional, academic, skilled or craft/artistic work and many of the remainder ran their own businesses in the service sector. During the Project there was a low incidence of unwaged households (10) and single parent families (6). There was a great mix of ethnic origin in the nursery. A third of the children came from ethnic minority groups

The beautiful garden is one of the setting's biggest assets

or came from homes where English was the second language of at least one parent.

Children attended either morning (9.00–11.30 am) or afternoon (12.45–3.15 pm) sessions, five days a week. Because of particular needs often arising from home circumstances, a few (up to five) children stayed all day and had lunch at nursery. The children in the two daily sessions were divided into three groups of 26 children, with a nursery teacher and nursery nurse in each group. Each group had its own suite of rooms with broadly the same equipment and facilities for the same activities. Each had areas with washable flooring, a large sink, a carpeted room and access to child-sized toilets and basins. The children stayed in their own rooms for the first half hour of the session and returned there for storytime in the last half hour. During the rest of the time they were free to play in any room or they could go outside as long as there was a member of staff out there. Two groups were housed on the ground floor, with shared cloakroom and toilets as well as the parents' room and a large kitchen. The third group was housed on the first floor, along with the office, staffroom and small kitchen.

STRATEGIES FOR WORKING TOGETHER

The EEL Project was introduced to the staff by two members of the EEL team and it quickly became apparent that its cycle of evaluation, action planning, development and reflection closely mirrored the nursery's own development process. This was based on the procedure for Development Planning for Schools set out by the local authority. During the Evaluation Stage of the Project, the EEL Support Worker spent two days a month in the nursery gathering data from documents, interviews and observations. All members of the staff and the Support Worker collaborated to gather evidence and through consultation built up an agreed picture of the quality of educational experience for all the children in the nursery. The resulting Evaluation Report highlighted a number of areas for development. Staff decided to focus on one area and, during their normal team meetings, produced ideas for an Action Plan, which the Support Worker collated and submitted for confirmation before the action commenced.

The first phase of the Action Plan was carried out in the term following the Evaluation Stage. During interviews and the composition of vignettes with the Support Worker, staff reflected on aspects of the action they had carried out. The Support Worker carried out a second set of observations after the Development Stage and the Final Report was submitted during the following term. Because of the processes already in place in the nursery, the cycle of evaluation and development continued after the period of the Project.

EVALUATING PRACTICE

The EEL Support Worker gathered information from nursery documents, observation of children, staff and activities, and interviews with parents, staff and children. These data were then considered in relation to the EEL ten dimensions of quality which provided a comprehensive picture of the quality of children's experience in the nursery.

The workshop layout of the classrooms fosters independence.

The nursery aimed to adhere to fundamental principles of good practice in early years education and provide a 'warm, secure learning environment'. The staff envisaged the curriculum as addressing children's social, emotional, intellectual, physical and spiritual development. Parents felt that the nursery provided their children with the 'foundation for all sorts of different subjects to prepare them for infant school'. Some anxiety was expressed that some children would be subjected to a different curricular emphasis when they transferred to their infant schools with concentration on the early acquisition of literacy skills.

While appreciating the value of the experiences the nursery offered, some parents were still uneasy that their children might be disadvantaged in an environment where acquiring the ability to read and write was seen as paramount.

The style of the nursery's approach to learning emphasised learning through doing, active involvement and playing and talking, and on developing self-esteem, good relationships, self-confidence and independence. The staff were confident of how to interpret these principles to guide their practice. The children should learn through 'active learning' and 'hands-on experience with opportunities to explore, experiment, investigate, record and predict'. The adult's role was described as that of a playmate, enabler and teacher whose tasks were 'observing, listening, discussing, reassuring', 'supporting, extending their knowledge' and 'skilled interaction'. The workshop layout of the classrooms, the accessibility of the provision and the organisation and planning of activities was seen as essential. 'Everything is laid out for them to select and put back' and this fostered independence.

Observation of target children, target activities and adult style showed that the children were learning in ways that were consistent with the aims and principles outlined by staff in the interviews and in nursery documentation. In the classroom, staff were able to spend most of their time talking to the children, extending their thinking, encouraging their efforts, easing turn-taking and managing conversations. Their role changed when supervising outside activities, partly because more attention had to be devoted to safety, and partly because the children's needs were different.

Thirty children were observed throughout the sessions during the Evaluation Stage. Children were chosen from the register at random, but ensuring that there were equal numbers of boys and girls in the 3 and 4 years age bands. Some children were very new to nursery, some were about to leave for infant school. From Figure 1.1 it can be seen that all groups showed a high level of Involvement, averaging just below level 4, with little difference between am/pm, boys/girls or 3/4 year olds.

In general, children were deeply involved in activities for most of the session, with very little 'milling around' or merely routine completion of tasks. The quality of child-to-child talk (often picking up themes from previous discussions with staff) and high levels of Involvement meant that the children enjoyed good learning experiences even without adult participation. Many children maintained their high levels of Involvement into tidy-up time. Some children even seemed to look forward to this flurry of purposeful activity and the opportunity to take responsibility for a task.

Four members of staff (two teachers and two nursery nurses) were observed

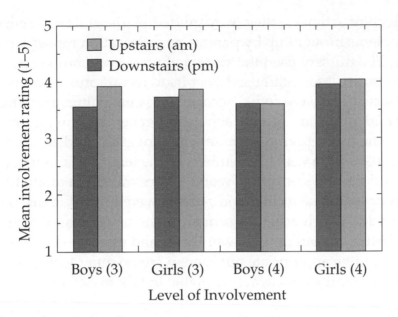

Figure 1.1   Involvement by age and gender

during morning and afternoon sessions in the Evaluation Stage. The data from all adults' observations were pooled to provide an overall picture of the adult behaviour within the nursery relating to three aspects of adult behaviour: Sensitivity, Stimulation and Autonomy. All adults presented very similar positive, patient and professional profiles. The most striking feature was the wealth of Stimulation from all members of staff. Conflicts and correction of behaviour were rare events, but were handled positively when they arose. The adults' style varied with activity. At the beginning the emphasis was on empathy and responsiveness as they greeted children and settled less confident children. Levels of stimulation rose during classroom activities, while outside play and tidy-up time required positive handling of rules, conflicts and behaviour. Storytime placed the emphasis on empathy, stimulation and positive handling of children's language. Some of the adults' talk was aimed at helping children manage their conversations, organising who would speak next, checking that everyone had heard a comment from a quieter member of the group. They also spent a lot of time explaining and describing to children what they were doing, and if they left an activity or could not respond to a request immediately, they explained why. Besides providing the children with models of verbal reasoning, this gave rise to a secure and reassuring atmosphere where the children's feelings and apprehensions were always being considered.

The staff planned the activities through weekly team meetings for each group. In selecting activities, they were guided by the children's current interests, problems brought up by parents or preparation for seasonal events and changes. The nursery used the system of nursery record keeping developed within the authority. Most staff used Post-its to record observations during sessions. Observations were coded according to curriculum area and noted in a file for that child alongside specific action and general planning implications.

Each term the teacher wrote an assessment of each child as a result of collaborative discussion with all members of the team and reference to the coded observations and samples of work. Before transition to infant school, a profile was written for each child and parents were invited to discuss the profile and sample folder, which was then sent on to the infant school. Some parents wondered whether an earlier review of their child's progress 'a chat, perhaps half-yearly' might be appropriate but there were no other formal sessions to discuss progress. Staff were always available to talk to parents after sessions if required.

The nursery teachers acted as team leaders in planning, assessment and record keeping, and had ultimate responsibility for their groups. During sessions, however, teacher and nursery nurse had equal roles, with equal involvement and interaction with children and with carrying out observations. Caring and cleaning up roles were shared, as was liaison with parents, each group operating very much as a team. The staff all voiced their commitment to constant discussion to monitor the appropriateness of activities and children's progress and to the continual review and assessment of their own work. Everyone emphasised maintenance of high standards in the nursery.

The staff and parents all thought the building offered a good physical environment for young children. The staff emphasised the importance of space both indoors and outdoors. They believed there should be suitable space around trays and tables, and sufficient space to allow easy opening of doors and use of equipment. It was felt that, in a perfect world, perhaps some of the rooms could be bigger. Parents valued the fact that the nursery was housed in a separate building, which made it safe and private.

The nursery placed relationships with adults and other children as central to the child's development and parents believed that their children needed a balance between kindness and care and fostering independence. Adults handled their interactions with the children in ways consistent with their aims to value individuals, foster independence and self-esteem. They were patient, warm and encouraging, and showed genuine interest in talking to the children, adding comments from their own experiences so that real conversations took place. They praised appropriately, showing sensitivity to the effort, care and persistence which had been put into an activity.

The nursery presented an atmosphere of cultural richness and diversity. There were family connections ranging across the five continents, with the result that children were more used to looking at themselves as part of a global family, than in seeing others as outsiders or strangers to their own culture. The staff aimed to make every child 'proud of their culture' and if any child was heard using racist language, this was taken up with that child's parents. Parents valued the cultural variety of the nursery and the way this promoted 'acceptance of other people's beliefs'. Equal treatment of boys and girls was an issue about which the parents interviewed (in this case all mothers) had strong views. There was 'no stereotyping, no judgment' about 'boys in beads' or girls doing woodwork. The staff supported the integration of children with special educational needs but felt that it was very important that extra staff were allocated for the target child so that she gained maximum benefit from her time at nursery and so that other children did not suffer from reduction in attention from staff.

Partnership with parents was started well before the child's first day at nursery. The nursery was involved with the local toddler group, which was run on a voluntary basis by a member of the governors. Children and parents were shown round the nursery when the child was registered and, during the term before the child commenced, the parent and child visited the nursery. A home visit was arranged, but only if parents were happy about it. During the 'gentle settling-in time' the child was gradually encouraged to spend time away from his parent's side until they were ready to say goodbye at the beginning of the session. Children engaged in mainly solitary play while they were settling into the nursery, but later most children played in groups of two, three or four, in parallel or cooperatively.

Parents were encouraged to accompany children on nursery outings and to help in the nursery by, for example, reading in mother tongue, playing musical instruments and cooking special food. Staff were keen that parents should understand what goes on at nursery, and used displays and posters to communicate their aims. They had also put on two open evenings, one general and one Hands-on Science evening.

All in all, the Evaluation Report presented a picture of a well-equipped, well-organised nursery offering a wide range of well-planned activities to a large number of children. The children showed a high level of independence and Involvement in their play and the commitment, skill and professionalism of all the staff was readily apparent. There was a good match between written policy, stated aims and actual practice. Everyone spoke with one voice and parents had picked up many of the nursery's aims for children's learning and development but were sometimes uncertain about the links between nursery activities and infant school.

ACTION PLANNING

The draft version of the Evaluation Report was first discussed with staff and a final version agreed. Following discussion with the deputy head, it became clear that it would be necessary to select short-term aims to work on for the remainder of the school year, and that other areas of development would be best left until the next school year when the changes in staff would have taken place and the new development plan was discussed.

The areas on which the nursery focused their Action Plan were:

- involvement of parents in record keeping and assessment

- helping parents to understand the aims of nursery education

- improving liaison with infant schools, including procedures for transition to infant schools, to maximise continuity of provision

- promoting the importance of good nursery practice to a wider public

- broadening the range and depth of early literacy activities and opportunities to develop these skills within the classroom.

It was decided that the nursery would focus on this last area – Early Literacy – for the first Development Stage, and that this action would be monitored by the Project. The Action Plan was clearly focused on developing this aspect of their provision.

Aims of the Action Plan

1   To raise the awareness of Early Literacy in staff and students
2   To give Early Literacy a higher profile in classroom activities
3   To help parents understand the relationship between nursery activities and learning to read and write.

Strategies

1   Review the range and methods of storytelling currently used within the groups
2   Use naturally occurring opportunities to talk to parents about the way Early Literacy develops
3   Review provision for development of Early Literacy skills in graphics area, role-play contexts and during painting, modelling and construction.

Action

1   In weekly team meetings:

- discuss ways of improving range, access to and organisation of books, and ways of varying storytelling

- discuss ways to note emerging literacy skills involved in, for example, drawing, painting, building.

2   Talk to parents about new emphasis on Early Literacy in classroom. Put up a chart to give examples of activities and the Early Literacy skills which can be developed from them. Talk at profile meetings about the importance of these skills in the processes of learning to read and write;

3   Set up role-play area for children to use writing in role-play setting;

4   Think about location of graphics area and relocate if necessary, for example move away from messy activities, make sure enough space provided;

5   Record stories as they develop out of children's paintings and constructions. Encourage children who have started to make own books.

A timetable for this action was drawn up.

IMPROVING PRACTICE

In weekly team meetings, the staff discussed ways of improving access to books, their range and organisation, and ways of varying storytelling. They also discussed ways to observe merging literacy skills involved in, for example, drawing, painting and building. A chart was put up in the staffroom so that each group could contribute ideas for activities and highlight the Early Literacy skills which could be developed from these activities.

Two main aspects of action then followed. Classrooms were reorganised and special activities arranged, while the staff ensured they were ready to respond to any aspects of Early Literacy which occurred in the normal range of classroom activities. Role-play areas were set up so that the children could use writing in role-play settings. One group had an office, one a shop with till receipts and all groups added magazines and telephone pads to their home corners. Graphics areas were relocated in some groups and a wider range of writing implements and paper were available in all groups.

Each group made friezes or set up small world or role-play activities after the children had particularly enjoyed listening to a story. One group visited a book shop and bought new books, while another visited an office. Class books were

Children often engaged in role play after listening to a story

made about recent visits or favourite stories. Children who started to make their own books were encouraged and their finished books were shown to the rest of the group and read at storytime. This generated great enthusiasm for book-making and book-making activities were then arranged in all groups. Because the spark which led to the enthusiasm for Early Literacy activities was different in each group, the activities which followed developed along different lines. One group concentrated on the physical skills of writing and experimented with different paper and writing implements. Another group became interested in different formats of books and made flap books and split books, while the third group showed more interest in the content of the book, its story line and the sequence of pictures. There was considerable cross-fertilisation of ideas, however, and children tried out activities they encountered in other groups.

REFLECTION ON ACTION

On return to the nursery after the Action Plan had been in force for two weeks, the sudden explosion of writing and book-making activity was evident from the moment of stepping through the door. There were displays of books which the children had made and graphics areas with blank books, lined paper or pens and ink. Children in the book corner were keen to 'read' to their friends and wrote 'notes' on message pads when they took phone calls in the home corner. Wall friezes and paintings had captions telling the story behind the picture.

In the first group, the children had first produced books that echoed current topics of interest, drawing pictures and either writing or opting for scribing from the adults. They had then experimented with ink and a wide variety of different writing materials and most had opted to produce writing rather than drawing. In the second group, the range of books produced showed the extent to which the children had become involved in the mechanics and structure of books. There were flaps which lifted to reveal surprises, zig-zag books and split books. Some children had started to add speech bubbles with words inside to their work, but most had preferred adults to scribe for them, despite the fact that this group had in fact produced quite a lot of emergent writing during the previous term. In the third group, after the introduction of the office area, there was an increase in the amount of writing in the graphics area. Following the decision to have an adult to support activity in the graphics area, sequences of pictures began to emerge and the children produced more 'story' as opposed to 'catalogue' books.

In all groups, the enthusiasm for book-making was carried over into activities at home as the children, proud of the books they had made at nursery, took them home and made more books with their parents. This, together with evidence from book-making activities displayed in the classrooms, promoted discussions on Early Literacy with parents. It was also possible to observe an increased confidence in children across the groups in storytelling, 'reading' and use of all graphics materials.

A second set of Involvement data was collected at the end of the Development Stage from 20 children (10 from the morning session of one group 10 from the afternoon session of another), with equal numbers of boys and girls observed. More 4 year olds than 3 year olds were observed (13 versus 7) but a number of these (8) had only recently had their 4th birthdays and this sample represented the age profile of the nursery at that point in the school year. There were many aspects of nursery life which differed since the first round of observations. It was summer and the children spent more time outside then they had in November and December. Most of the children had been attending nursery for over a term and so were familiar with nursery routines and activities. One set of observations included a trip to a nature centre. There had also been changes of staff and students. It is not possible to assess the extent to which any of these factors affected the levels of Involvement recorded during this second phase. There was a slight increase in mean level of Involvement (3.79 to 3.98). The overriding picture remained one of high levels of Involvement throughout the nursery sessions.

Two members of staff were also observed during the same period and all the differences mentioned in the discussion of the results of the Involvement assessment apply to the observation of adult style. Nonetheless, the results of the second round of observations show a very similar positive, patient and professional profile to that observed earlier. The level of Stimulation was still high; this was particularly apparent during the trip to the nature centre.

The staff felt that their aims had been realised and they were delighted with the children's enthusiastic and creative response to the activities and changes in classroom organisation which had been carried out. The children gained in confidence that they too could be storytellers, authors and publishers. Parents became involved in helping their children with Early Literacy skills and developed an understanding of how these skills were laying the foundations for reading and writing. Fitting in as it did with the school's Development Plan and with previous activities in each group, the Early Literacy Action Plan was a great success.

ISSUES FOR FURTHER REFLECTION

This Case Study described how a team of teachers and nursery nurses in an LEA nursery school worked in partnership with an EEL Support Worker to gather evidence about the quality of their provision and to develop an Action Plan for improvement. Their Action Plan focused on:

- raising the awareness of Early Literacy in staff and students;

- giving Early Literacy a higher profile in classroom activities;

- helping parents understand the relationship between nursery activities and learning to read and write.

The processes they went through in achieving this improvement in their practice raise a number of important questions for discussion by those who work both within this type of setting and beyond.

1   Nursery schools are often viewed as 'centres of excellence' for other providers. Why is this and how might this role be further developed?
2   Why do you think parents expressed some anxiety about the acquisition of reading and writing skills in the nursery? How might these anxieties be addressed by practitioners?

3   The staff at this nursery used Post-its to record their ongoing observations. What other strategies are there?

4   What are the different roles of teachers and nursery nurses? How might both develop their role within the team?

5   This nursery placed a great emphasis on equal opportunities issues. How were they addressing the issues in this nursery?

6   What would you have added to the Action Plan for Early Literacy? What would you have changed?

7   What are the aspects of provision in this nursery school that deserve wider application?

2 CASE STUDY TWO – A FAMILY CENTRE

Tina Bruce, Margy Whalley, Katie Mairs, Cath Arnold and the Centre team

CONTEXT

This chapter is an attempt to capture the essence of what was happening in this setting. What shines through is that this setting was not a place at all. It was a process which aimed towards the product 'quality'. Neither the process nor the product are easy to articulate since everything was in a constant state of flow.

The changes brought about by the process were inevitable, because people and buildings, for all kinds of reasons and through all sorts of circumstances, inevitably change. But there was a strong undercurrent through the flow which pulled those working there to seek ways to bring about better lives for the children and their families. It has been a privilege to try to capture the essence of this remarkable place.

Getting to know the centre

It might be helpful to begin with thoughts from the people who used the Centre. It took time for parents or visitors to get to know about the multipurposes of the building and the community in action. Different parents related to it in different ways. An experienced mother, whose older child had special educational needs, and who had a daughter in the nursery said,

> I thought it was organised chaos at first. I thought, what's going on here? As you get used to it you begin to say, yes, that's the home corner, that's the wet area. There is everything here for them. Amongst the chaos, there are quiet corners screened off, and quiet places in there.

One new parent was helped to use the Centre by the Health Visitor. She attended the Centre regularly, and her totally blind son went with his helper to the nursery, or with her to aromatherapy sessions and to use the toy library. He loved to go first to the soft play room before he went into the nursery. She reported that at home he would bang on the door all the time,

Making an arch

> *They helped him to stop. It was like a team of help . . . I don't worry when I leave him. He is always fine. He gets lots of cuddles, the kids love him here. The staff want him. He is not missing out . . . you feel involved. They tell me what he had for dinner. At nursery he drinks from a beaker and feeds himself. He stays for lunch, sometimes, to give me a break. It's a great help. They let him do what he wants to do. I am glad though. They do things without forcing. When he goes along the corridor, he knows where he is going. He goes happily.*

We can sense how this mother was reassuring herself. She was not yet fully settled in to this community.

Although one father did not know the detailed workings of the Centre, he knew his Family Worker, who visited regularly at home. She visited with her folder, to show what his daughter had done.

> *You have a say . . . they do listen. She gets covered in paint. When I meet her I get her changed. I can't walk up the road with her like that. They say children need to*

learn and be free to do things in nursery. They need respect because it is not an easy job. I've got an enlarged photo at home now. (It was of his daughter gardening on an outing.)

Everyone was valued in this setting, whether a successful businesswoman, drug addict, from a minority ethnic group, disabled, from a dysfunctional family, lonely, poor or unhealthy. The community was based on respect for persons. This was realised through the value placed on enabling access to anyone in the community and, out of this, the empowerment that was given to everyone to move forward. These were not ideals with no action. The vision was constantly strived towards in real and active ways. There was an emphasis on assertiveness training, child and adult protection, physical and mental awareness training and meetings for staff, parents and children on matters of race, gender and disability. These meetings helped to inform, challenge stereotypes and encourage open discussion. These issues were directly focused upon, and were also embedded implicitly in, the work of the Centre.

The physical environment

This was a steel working community until 'the candle went out'. Links with Glasgow were strong and it was often described as 'up the road'. The building was an ex-secondary school and clinic and continued to have multipurposes and functions in the 1990s. Groups that operated in the building included the Playgroup, Fathers' Group, Women Survivors' Support Group, Understanding Nursery Education Group, Aromatherapy and Massage for Babies, Poetry Group, Parents' Groups for children with special educational needs, and a Snoezelen, together with a group run by Health Visitors for parents who had experienced stillbirth or miscarriage.

On one day the following were observed:

Corridor
Tent, small Lego, books, photo books, umbrella and theme bags, message boxes, flip chart to draw on.

Main room
Computers, office, home corner (upstairs and downstairs), large books, sofa and chair, rocking horse, snacks café, display of shelves and oriental massive world, play mat, map, children's maps on wall and photos, gutters and roads on walls, garages, wood and small cars, Duplo cars, aquarium, potted plants, messy area, muddy mixing paints, tea urn and water tray, wooden steps, things for water tray, shelves and trolley with boats in tray, sea shells, tea sets, reptiles, low sink,

glue, scissors, collage, beads for sorting, sieves and colanders, saucepans, unit blocks, display of building books, for example one of a Greek temple.

Outside

Pulley, sink, trikes for one, trikes for groups, tyres, buckets, climbing frames, bats and balls, hoops, screen and materials, house (upstairs and downstairs), milk crates, tennis rackets, netball goal, tyre on wheels, broom, rubbish bin, pipes and guttering, peat, wheelbarrows, large dominoes, washing line to hang paintings, collage table and paint table, slides, pot for water, carrying tray, gravel in the large sand tray (containing buckets and spades), large tip-up lorry, metal buckets, sponge bowls.

Indoors

Large blocks, wooden boxes, buckets made into a car and steering wheel, office (with screen around it), home area, rocking horse, sofa, snack bar (self-service), water with urn, large magnets on a metal board on the floor, plants and fish tanks, globes on a floor mat, unit blocks, workshop area, paint mixing, music or chime bars on a large stand, garage and cars, books, display of books, bricks and buildings, mixing cornflour in bowls, ice lumps, adults would read stories on request, grouptime (discussions, songs, stories), message boards, parachute.

Staffing

Great emphasis was placed on training, both for parents and staff, and it showed. As a parent commented in an interview,

> I think the training they do is very important – the specialist training they do. It helps them like their work and like the children. The enthusiasm rubs off on the children. It is just brilliant. If the staff do not like what they are doing, the quality goes.

This mother, with two others (one a Family Worker in a nursery) ran a group called 'In Betweeners – Messy play', for children of 1–3 years of age at the Centre.

Parents felt that they could develop through groups and the same was the case for members of staff. During the time the Support Worker worked with staff in the Centre she observed several very nervous new members of staff grapple and struggle, identify their training needs with their supervisor, act on them and develop with startling rapidity. The staff had a range of starting points: NVQ, BTEC, NNEB, qualified graduate training Nursery/Infant Teacher. They were highly motivated to work here; they had chosen this Centre because they wanted to be part of something with a nationwide reputation for excellence and they understood what it was to develop and learn, and what hard work this entailed. This approach was adopted for the staff's own sake, but also importantly, for the sake of the better work they would be able to do with children, families and colleagues in the Centre. There was excitement and commitment, enjoyment of their work, but never complacency or arrogance, because there was always an awareness of what needed to be done next. A rolling programme of training on different areas, such as observation of schemata, separation anxiety between parents and children and assertiveness were offered with regularly visiting trainers. Some training was based on individual needs and some on team needs.

Above all, there was absolute respect for the family. The staff were encouraged to see themselves as enablers and facilitators for each family, and in particular, for the children in their family group. They recognised that their role did not mean taking over the family, or compensating for deficiencies in dysfunctional families, or telling parents how to be good parents. They wanted to work with the family, helping the family to identify its needs and the direction to take, helping families to help themselves and rallying and co-ordinating support networks to bring this about.

STRATEGIES FOR WORKING TOGETHER

Collaboration and partnership were at the heart of the work of this Centre. The staff had developed a number of strategies to realise this mode of operation.

Working with parents

Parents at the Centre were sometimes initially of the view that there should be more discipline, or less mess, or more sitting children down. One father expressed his concern about the need for children to know right from wrong. He said,

> The good thing about Corby is that the Scottish element has made it a town to live in – it's a community from the steel works – but you still have to look after yourself ... Corby is a place where children need discipline. I don't know how the staff in the Centre encourage a dominant character and suppress aggression in it ... I went to the meeting 'Learning to be Strong'. I didn't appreciate how grown up they are. He (his 4 year old son) grasped what they were trying to teach. Definitely a benefit.

Another father thought the good thing about family grouptime was that there was within the Centre a

> *modicum of what you need to sit still. But not a lot of that. It is too early for strong discipline. Later in school they need to sit for a period of time. Here they have the freedom to walk about, but an element of discipline too. When they go to the soft room in a group, it teaches them to be a team. It is a bit short of a bouncy castle – but not actually a sport. That comes when they start school. It is too early to do that here. Too much emphasis on winning.*

Another father thought that children benefit as they play together and figure things out together, so they are prepared to leave the Centre when the time comes. He commented that his son wanted to read and write and he thought that the Centre had given his son a start before primary education. He also appreciated the system of the Family Worker and thought it was important that his son was with a Family Worker who was a man and from a minority ethnic group. He valued the special books, which helped parents and staff to analyse what his son did 'half an hour at a time. Otherwise you can miss the wood for the trees'.

He was very clear that,

> *By the time they start school, unless they love paper and swotting, they get out of it, then, when they leave, they wish they hadn't. There is a fine line at the Centre to teach children and bring out what is in them already. He would not be the kid he is today if he had not gone down there.*

He summed up the Centre,

> *It's modern in approach. It is run like a modern business with a Managing Directress who is flexible and friendly. Not too familiar, but you feel able to talk to her. Other schools could use the same approach and do a lot better and try to get the parents' involvement.*

This father took a while to tolerate the messy paint, and then developed strategies to deal with it (a change of clothes to walk through the public streets without shame). Parents were aware of both the subject areas being taught and the experiences through which children were introduced to them. A mother commented in her interview,

She's into writing. Everything has her name on it. She is already writing letters down and says 'What's that?' You write letters and she knows what they say, with words she asks 'What does that say?' She says 'That letter is in my name.'

A mother of a child with special educational needs appreciated the soft play room, trampoline, water at the sink, musical instruments, storytime and feelings (ready for braille) and the way staff were speaking to her son all the time, 'telling him where things are, and what things are'.

The pleasure of writing

She was pleased with the outside visits to farms and the chance her son had to feel the animals. She commented that he had become a water baby at the swimming baths where the staff take him.

Another mother who took an active part in the Centre thought that at the Centre children,

> learn through play without realising it. They learn social skills to get on with other people. It's OK not to like someone, as long as there is no fighting.

She was proud that her son had written CAT upside down so that she could read it.

> He loves reading. I like the way they have stories with groups. They get a feeling of independence – they make their own snacks in the cafe. . . . There is so much variety. It seems to fit every child, and without realising it they are learning . . . they do Science – pulleys. A few weeks later he used a rope and pulled his sister's pushchair upstairs. A lot of what he wants to know is Physics.

Using a pulley

She attended the Understanding Nursery Group led by a Family Worker and commented on the way that the staff worked with the children,

The adults are there if they need them, but they don't interfere. They observe a lot. When I ask what he has done, they always know.

From these examples emerge some of the essential features of the way the staff worked with parents. The discussions with parents on discipline, rich experiences with paint, learning and physics are clearly shown. The way parents and staff valued training and becoming informed about children's learning, and sharing what they learn, is also clear. There was real commitment to training for staff and parents, using external courses and trainers, and not a sole reliance on in-house training. This helped all the adults at the Centre to observe, support and extend children's development and learning and to provide the children with rich, broad, deep and relevant experiences.

Home-made interest books

These were made with the children. They showed the work being done with simple annotation and photographs. These were left in corridors or on interest tables, at child height so that everyone could see them and refer to them. They were in constant use by parents, children, staff and visitors.

Everyone has a say

Staff, including administrative staff, catering and caretaking services, parents and children, all had their say through meetings, courses and documents. There was a strong but open leadership, which acted as a catalyst, enabler and setter of boundaries at different points. Discussions were lively, abrasive and frank. Each member of staff was supported through a process of supervision which is based on the social work model. In this way nothing festered. During these supervision sessions, staff 'interviewed' each other, making life histories, emotional maps, addressing particular areas, appraisal, nurture, tutorial and complaining. A member of staff commented,

If I perceived a training need for me I would get it eventually. I have moved very quickly in terms of professional and personal development – bereavement counselling, more group training.

Parents are also involved in meetings, and they access the setting through their Family Worker. A parent commented in an interview,

She has her special book. I put my tuppence worth in. She likes dressing up, sparkly shoes. They let me take them home. I bring them back again. They don't mind. Then the dressing-up can continue at home.

Parents could also turn to any member of staff, and so could the children. Children were involved as much as possible. There were special books which they made with their Family Worker to help to articulate their needs, fascinations and deep learning. These child-profile books were called 'A Celebration of My Achievements'. They were held in locked filing cabinets in the classroom. Children and parents could (and did) request to see them at any time. When children left, the record became parent-held, and was taken to show the receiving school. Receiving schools reported their delight in them as a good way of bonding with new children and parents entering statutory schooling. The value of the special books was evident in the way that children showed visitors the Centre and offered to share their special books. Each child regularly worked with his Family Worker to develop his book.

The level of involvement and respect accorded to the children was clear. Children see adults in many meetings and observe closely what goes on. When the children came for their group interview for the EEL Project they asked, 'Where is the coffee and biscuits?' (which was quickly organised by the staff) and one child said at the beginning, 'Why don't we go round and say who we are?'

Formulating centre policies as a team

Using a vast range of mechanisms, everyone in the Centre played a part in formulating policy in some way. There was an usual degree of pride, commitment and ownership in the Centre. Staff respected each other and received assertiveness training (as did parents and children), so that debates were not aggressive or bullying in tone. But there were regularly situations where policies, ideas, feelings and relationships were reviewed, bashed about, developed or changed. However, deep down, everyone was clear about the limits, and if the senior management team argued against or for something, it was taken very seriously by the staff.

In practice, new initiatives and the identification of areas of strength or weakness in the Centre were usually led from the senior management team – but not always. There was no fear on their part to lean if required, and in the same way, they did not feel threatened or defensive about the thrashing and bashing about of ideas, because of regular in-service training in management. Everything was up for review and discussion.

Keeping careful records by staff and parents

Records were an important part of work in the Centre. The EEL Project served as a valuable enhancer of progress and record keeping, planning and observation of children. The strategies adopted were:

- child profiles, in the form of special books, which included carefully recorded observations by staff, families and parents;

- specially developed forms to record observations;

- the requirement that staff take two or three examples of observations to each supervision meeting with their senior manager to be discussed in detail;

- discussion of parents' observations with the Family Worker during home visits;

- weekly plans, worked out as a team at a weekly meeting;

- daily plans which allowed for spontaneous events to be quickly followed up by staff so that they were responsive to individual children;

- special forms devised for weekly and daily planning;

- long-term plans developed out of observations of children. For example, identification of a child's schemata might lead to a 'possible line of development' or PLOD chart.

Planning children's experiences

Suitable, appropriate and educationally worthwhile experiences were planned in the light of observations. Links were made with areas of knowledge and understanding, including links with areas of the National Curriculum, where appropriate and obvious, although this was not legally required with this age group. The planning process was continuous and permeated the whole day.

Every child was greeted as he or she came in and if necessary, the adult would see that the child linked with his Family Worker. All adults were on the alert for 'their' children and 'their' parents. Staff saw this as a time to relate to parents, and so the first part of a session had a very chatty feel. Activities such as cooking took place a little later, when parents had settled their children in this relaxed way. Children chose what they did, care being taken to see that each child was offered the full range of experiences available. Some adults were on a

Enjoying a book together

rota to be in a designated area and the wet area, the corridor and the outdoor areas were always staffed. Other staff were free to move about. However, despite the free movement and conversation, it was an accepted rule that no-one interrupted an adult talking to, or working with, a child.

Staff would invite children to take part in activities they had planned with a particular individual in mind. The child was never forced, instead the planning was modified! Children often did not need an invitation. They seemed to seek out the experiences that 'spoke' to them. For example, Nina transported, enveloped and transformed material wherever she could. It was no surprise that she headed for the mixtures table on arrival, where she found green splodgy cornflour, powder, water, bowls, ladles, spatulas, spoons, a range of lentils, an urn and a bowl of green water. An adult was in this area and supported Nina as she mixed and transported materials with bowls, spoons and scoops, functioning at a symbolic representational level,

We are making dinner. No. We are making ice cream. We are going to make ice cream for our pudding.

Later, she said to another girl,

We eat the dinner up first, and I have nearly finished mine.

She dropped the sludge into a bowl. The match between schemata and activity held Nina's attention. She stayed in this area for more than 20 minutes, observed by staff. The cake theme is recurrent. In their subsequent planning the staff linked this activity with science, transforming materials, role-play and cooking. This was written on to a PLOD chart and curriculum area extensions were planned with Nina in mind.

Whilst some events occurred because of advanced planning, arising out of observations, not all did. For example, Janet spent more than 20 minutes in the home corner, savouring, having it and an adult all to herself. She transported and set up a sequence to do the washing, taking dressing-up clothes and putting them in the washing machine, then hanging them over a rack (a clothes horse). The adult supported her, seizing a teaching moment, by staying and talking with her as she played with 'wash day'.

When the nursery was in operation the needs of the children were paramount. During the last 20 minutes of both the morning and afternoon sessions, the children went with their Family Worker into groups. Each group had its own area, and each Family Worker had a display board, which was her or his responsibility. Grouptime involved stories, songs and discussions and parents often joined them. Children had lunch in a beautiful dining room with their named photograph as a place mat on the table. They loved to discuss what they were doing in the photo with visitors, staff and children. The office staff, the cleaner and other staff on lunch duty ate with the children. There was an emphasis on nutritious, enjoyable, shared eating and good conversation.

This description of how particular children use the nursery, and how it is geared to meet their needs, demonstrates the emphasis on, and benefits of, working together.

EVALUATING PRACTICE

The EEL Project was used by the Centre as a way of 'taking stock' much more tangibly than before. It helped staff to see good practice, and to enhance it further, rather than changing practice. The Project facilitated the continuation of the work on record keeping. It enlarged the mechanism staff used for observations of children. Observations were better used to inform planning.

The levels of Involvement were high throughout the Centre, but the EEL Project revealed a slight dip at grouptime. Staff identified this as something to be incorporated into the Action Plan, alongside a continuation of the work already underway on record keeping and extension in support of learning. The Involvement Scale was the basis of discussion at a subsequent training day. The observations and levels of Involvement were discussed and staff brought the special books of children who had been observed using the Involvement Scale. The EEL Support Worker added notes to the back of some of the charts to enhance what had been observed. This again demonstrates how the staff sought feedback, wanted training and acted on it. The observations at the end of grouptimes revealed that there was variation in the groups as far as the children's Involvement was concerned. It seemed that songs, stories and a cracking pace kept Involvement high. A swift gathering of the group and going straight into song appeared to lead to more Involvement by the children. At other times the consistent approach of the Centre staff was the most noticeable factor in determining the Involvement level of the children. In grouptimes what was offered was more varied, and the children's Involvement varied accordingly.

An example of a child in grouptime illustrated the issue for the staff. Lizzie (3 years old) did the actions when the Family Worker sang 'Wind the Bobbin'. She smiled as she imitated. The Family Worker immediately moved to the next song 'Where Are My Currant Buns?'. Lizzie was totally involved. She smiled, counted out loud, and did all the actions. Setting a good pace, the Family Worker had led the session by introducing two songs known to the group of children, swiftly one after the other. Having got the group's involvement, she then opened it up. She invited the children, 'What shall we sing now?' The general cry was for the 'Bobbins' again. This time every child joined in. The Family Worker then said, keeping the pace, 'Let's do one we haven't done before'. The head of nursery had just joined the group and suggested 'Sandy Girl'. Lizzie was at level 5 Involvement throughout.

ACTION PLANNING

At the end of each morning and afternoon during the Evaluation Stage the EEL Support Worker had informally given instant feedback to the staff and parents, showing them the forms she had filled in and talking them through what they showed. At the end of the Evaluation the Staff and Support Worker met for a whole day's in-service with a focus on feedback. The emphasis was on individual children and how they used the Centre. From this discussion the Action Plan emerged, and was activated from that time in the thinking of the staff (48 hours before the end of term). This meant that staff returning after the fortnight's summer break were considering how to implement the Action Plan straight away. At subsequent meetings the staff and the Support Worker reflected on and planned the next stage of action. There was also regular communication by fax and the Support Worker joined weekly staff meetings in September, October, November and January (four visits). Everyone felt that having the Support Worker as someone from outside, but on the edge of the Centre, was of great importance in helping them to see in perspective. They felt that this was too difficult to do on a day-to-day basis, and required outside help.

The Action Plan

Enhancement of record keeping, making observations of children and how to act on these observations, was not a new initiative. The Support Worker was already the in-service trainer (known in the Centre as 'the Pedagogue') and had been invited on a regular basis to work with staff on developing record keeping since 1991. Therefore the EEL Project did not identify a new need for the Centre. It confirmed a need that the Centre had already identified and was working on. However, it gave added mechanisms and strategies, as well as reaffirming the use of annotated photographs and supporting the major emphasis on child observation.

The Action Plan contained the following objectives:

1   Records of individual children to be further developed by:

- using all our work together on records and schema keeping

- developing participation in the EEL Project, especially the Child Involvement Scale.

Note: The Centre had a day's in-service with the EEL Support Worker looking at the findings of the Child Involvement and Target Child Observations. There followed a second day's in-service together looking at schemata in relation to record keeping. The Support Worker received a fax during a staff meeting requesting clarification of one or two observations which the staff were discussing. The Support Worker was able to supply instant feedback via the fax machine.

2   Staff should link even more supervision sessions with senior managers so as to make maximum progress in observation techniques and recording of children in their family group.

3   Support one member of staff to:

- develop her work on schemas

- follow through a group of children into Primary School

- link with the EEL Project

- ensure she has ownership of her MA!

4   Focus on grouptime at the end of the sessions since this was identified as the time when children are least involved. It was recognised that this is not a serious problem; it was simply a case of building on good to make it excellent.

Improving Practice

Putting the Action Plan into operation required the cooperation of everyone at the Centre. The various action initiatives had a number of elements and each raised issues which had to be tackled by the staff. These are laid out in the following analysis of what happened during the Development Stage of the Project.

Record keeping

- Staff turnover needed thought because this had implications for the continuity of work. Induction of new staff was seen as a major issue.

- The need to be more alert to the importance of writing down an observation as well as the importance of discussion was noted. This was not easy in a busy setting. Indeed it provided a great challenge, but the staff felt they had tightened up observation techniques.

- The importance of senior staff in their role as supervisors was highlighted. Reports from all the staff showed that they feel their records are developing through sharing the process during supervision.

- Providing regular feedback to parents was essential. Comments from staff showed that parents found it exciting to see the observations of their child.

- Observations revealed the stamina of little children. This was useful when looking at the purpose of activities at the end of grouptimes.

- Weekly meetings were enriched by written observations being brought to them and shared, induced and planned in a more rigorous way.

- Training days became a crucial part of the development. New staff 'found a voice' more easily in the team by having an outsider to facilitate the record keeping development. It helped new staff feel empowered to contribute.

- It was evident that the child's continuity with 'what happened today' needed to be respected the next day.

- It was agreed that extensions of learning needed to be appropriate and well thought-out.

Grouptimes

Grouptime was viewed as a special time for the children, and it formed the only fixed point in their session. This routine was seen to be especially important for children who often had no reliable patterns in their lives. The staff saw grouptime as providing a chance to:

- talk about what they had done that morning or afternoon

- hear what each child has to say so each child feels valued

- celebrate birthdays or special events

- share good news and sad news

- listen to others

- withdraw from a large group

- develop a small, peer group identity, as in the Italian nurseries which staff have visited regularly.

They identified and tried to implement a code of practice for grouptime. This contained the following suggestions for the staff:

- Withdraw into a small, comfortable area.

- Have a boundary about children staying there. It is the only time when the children are asked to stay in one place. (Obviously there are children who cannot cope with this.)

- Ensure children know where they should go and that they should take some responsibility for getting the area ready. If it changes they should be told in good time and, if they want to negotiate to go with someone else, this must be checked with a colleague.

- Encourage the same person each time to take the group. Try to prearrange who has your children, and that it is always the same person who takes your place so that the children know the person and do not feel powerless if the Family Worker cannot be there.

- Use songs, finger rhymes, drama, movement, dance, conversation, stories, puppets and so on.

- Remember that this time is very precious and needs to be planned to get the most out of it. Obviously numbers affect what is possible and appropriate.

The staff worked hard to put this agreed code into practice with the children.

Boundaries for staff

They also developed some guidelines for other areas.

- For outside play: if there are sufficient staff, we should reflect children's schemata and preoccupations in the outside play, i.e. the under-cover area can be planned and staffed in the same way as an area like blockplay or computer. If there are not enough staff, set out either nothing in the under-cover area and make a creative outside area, or on a very low cover day, stick to bikes outside.

- Cover arrangements: the principle is that only one member of the nursery staff is out at any one time. There needs to be some extra help with snacks, perhaps the kitchen assistant.

REFLECTION ON ACTION

Developing and implementing the Action Plan has been like a never-ending journey. The journey began before the EEL Project as the Support Worker in this setting had already worked regularly with staff and parents for three years. However, EEL has given everyone tangible evidence of the value and quality of their approach, and has certainly helped everyone involved to become more articulate and better focused. It has felt like outside appreciation of the work which has been done over 12 years, and has contributed towards the energy of staff to make the next 12 years develop and flourish.

Grouptime at the end of sessions, and what is now called 'community time' just before lunch, has been reviewed and acted upon. Records have been developed organically with adjustments being made constantly to fine-tune the system. Records of individual children and the organisation and planning of what is offered to children have become a real system.

The next priority will be to create a more effective system for new staff to grasp everything as easily as possible. The emphasis on staff supervision by senior management and help with observation techniques proved useful in this respect. So are classroom notices showing the 'network for learning' for each child, which the parents find useful. The incorporation of the Child Involvement Scale into the record keeping system also helped staff. The next step will be to increase further their depth of knowledge about:

- child development (schemata, etc.)

- curriculum areas (for example physics, forces, etc.)

and to link the two effectively.

Through the EEL Project, quality control has become a focus in a very tangible way and it will continue to be a priority in developing the Centre's future.

ISSUES FOR FURTHER REFLECTION

This Case Study described how a team of Family Centre workers, parents and children worked through a collaborative process to evaluate and develop their Centre. The EEL Support Worker helped them to focus their attention on three aspects of their provision:

- record keeping and observations of children

- grouptime

- staff development.

The processes they went through in achieving this improvement in their practice raise a number of important questions for discussion by those who work both within this type of setting and beyond.

1   The staff in this Centre collected evidence systematically and honestly about their strengths. What do you feel they could particularly celebrate?

2   This Centre had taken to heart the concept of 'improving on previous best'. Do you feel improvement is always possible, whatever the context?

3   The staff in this setting were strong and had the confidence to be self-critical. What are the factors which create this climate or inhibit it?

4   How did the setting help to foster and develop their teamwork?

5   There was great stress on staff development in this setting. How important do you feel this is? What structures had they put in place to support this emphasis?

6   What are the challenges of working together with parents? How had this Centre tackled them? What strategies had they put in place?

7   Why are observations of both children and staff important? How were these gathered and used to help the staff in this Centre?

8   What is the purpose of small grouptime? How helpful do you feel their code of practice for improving this was? What more might they have done?

9   How far do you feel the role of the outside EEL Support Worker was essential to the evaluation and development process? What characterised this role? Who might perform this function?

3 Case Study Three – A Private Day Nursery

Janet Dye

Context

This setting was a private day nursery organised by a Management Committee of parents. It catered for up to eighteen babies, from 3 to 24 months of age, and 32 children of 2 to 5 years of age. Babies and children could attend on a full- or part-time basis and fees were paid accordingly. The nursery was open all year round, apart from weekends, bank holidays and a week at Christmas. It opened at 8.30 am and closed at 5.30 pm. Morning sessions were from 8.30 am to 1.00 pm and afternoons were from 1.30 pm to 5.30 pm. In fact, most children and babies arrived between 8.30 and 9 am and were collected between 4.00 and 4.30 pm. Only four or five children and babies stayed until 5.30 pm.

Most of the children lived in the area, though several came from up to 40 miles away. The majority of the children were white, with a few from ethnic minorities, and most had mature language development. Their parents were interested in education and they worked in a university town while their children were in the nursery. Most children attended all year round, with only two or three weeks' absence for holidays. Almost half the children had been in the nursery since they were three months old.

The physical environment

The day nursery was situated in a quiet town road of large mature houses, some of which had been acquired for institutional use. The nursery and grounds occupied the site of a large house plot. The building was purpose built, light and modern. Inside there was a central playroom, which was also used for meals and snacks, with a small quiet area for group work and stories. A smaller playroom was used by 2, 3 and 4 year olds and had easy access to the outdoor area. There were also two babyrooms, each providing for nine babies under 2 years. The babyrooms had outdoor access and changing and bathroom areas nearby. The older children had their own toilet and washing facilities. There was a small kitchen where the catering contractor prepared meals. A staffroom and small office for the head and administrator completed the internal accommodation.

Outside, there were paved and grassed areas, shrubs, gardens, fixed climbing apparatus, a sandpit, a sheltered verandah and storage for outdoor equipment. There was car parking for staff and visitors and all approaches were secure with high gate fastenings. There were open grassed spaces, local shops and the river within a quarter of a mile of the nursery. The city centre was half a mile away.

The nursery was generally well equipped with materials for indoor and outdoor activities. Space was limited but the staff made good use of the attractive setting.

Staffing

The nursery was staffed by 14 adults, including the head and a part-time administrator. The head and four playroom staff were qualified nursery nurses with additional qualifications in social care, first aid and adult education. Two nursery assistants had City and Guilds qualifications in family and community

The high adult:child ratios allowed the staff to work with small groups of children

care. The playroom was staffed by six adults on a shift system, including one who only worked with the 4 year olds. Most of the staff had worked in the nursery for several years. Sometimes NNEB and work experience students helped in the nursery. Parents occasionally helped by sharing a skill or taking a group for music.

Organisation of the nursery

The head of the nursery had given considerable attention to curriculum and organisation in recent years. She had discussed her written study of the curriculum with the Management Committee and staff in order to make plans for necessary change and development. At the time there were no specific curriculum documents or plans relating to the education and care of the children in the nursery. However, staff aimed to provide for the main curriculum areas of experience covering human and social learning, language and literacy, mathematics, science and technology, physical education and creative and aesthetic education. Children's records were at an early stage of development. Few visits were arranged and invitations for visitors to share a skill were few. Curriculum planning was carried out within a generally agreed framework of what was regarded as normal nursery practice and normal nursery activities. The children chose from the activities made available by the staff. One member of staff supervised in a general way, leaving the others to work with particular groups of selected children and to set up the next activity. Activities included work with sand or water, painting, dough or printing, large and small construction, home corner play, book corner, drawing, table-top puzzles and games.

At weekly half-hour staff meetings, the organisation of particular aspects of the curriculum were discussed and staff responsibilities agreed. The activities for the children of 2 to 5 years were planned by the playroom leader supervised by the head. Sometimes the children's work incorporated a topic or theme. The playroom leader decided the focus for the next week within the term plan, reviewed past work, discussed topics or special activities and allocated staff responsibilities. These were then recorded and topic webs were produced. Staff breaks, lunchtime routines and rotas for outdoor play were also decided. As the nursery was open for long hours throughout the year, staff also worked in shifts so appropriate holiday breaks also had to be agreed. One member of staff had particular responsibility for the 4 year olds. She organised activities including writing, number, reading, drawing and using the computer, which were considered helpful to prepare children for school. There were no opportunities for group visits to children's future schools as they went to many different ones.

The children's day began between 8.30 and 9.00 am, when their parents and carers brought them into the nursery and they started with indoor activities. At 9.45 clearing up by adults and children began, ready for milk and biscuits to be served to all children at 10.00 in the main playroom. At 10.30 outdoor play was arranged for all children until 11.00, when washing was supervised. Stories were then told in two groups until 11.30, when lunch was set up and served by staff, taking until 12.30. Following this there were taped songs and stories for all until 12.50, when the children were encouraged to lie on the floor and rest, while some were taken home. Few children actually managed to sleep or rest. At 1.15 pm another story was read until 1.30 when the afternoon children arrived. From 1.30 to 2.20 activities were available indoors. At 2.20 these activities were cleared up by the children and adults and from 2.30 to 3.00 there was outdoor play for all. At 3.00 outdoor things were put away, children used the washroom, and songs and rhymes were led by the staff, followed by tea in the main room at 3.30 to 4.00. At 4.00 there were table-top activities in the playroom until 4.30. Most children were collected by 4.30. Those remaining had a story, then rested, used the computer, looked at books or drew. The last children were collected by 5.30.

STRATEGIES FOR WORKING TOGETHER

The EEL Support Worker discussed participation in the project with the nursery head, who then obtained full support from the Management Committee. The Support Worker then met with the nursery staff, including some of the babyroom staff, to discuss the project aims and methods, timetable and the cooperation needed. All the adults working with children aged 2 to 5 agreed to participate in the Project and were appropriately supported by the staff working with the babies. They hoped they would be given time to carry out observations.

A timetable for the Evaluation Stage was agreed to be completed in six to eight weeks, including interviews, Child Tracking observations, and these were to be carried out by the EEL Support Worker. Once work had begun, several staff said they were willing to carry out observations and interviews with the children. The headteacher supplied copies of the parents' booklet, newsletter, nursery plan, an outline list of equipment and details of staffing, admission policy and routines to the Support Worker.

Interviews with the staff were carried out informally at lunchtime and after their working sessions. Interviews and discussions with parents were conducted when they brought or collected their children. Sometimes several parents were interviewed together as they preferred this and their time was limited. An extended interview with the head took place as part of the working day. The children were interviewed informally in twos and threes by the EEL Support Worker in the quiet area or staffroom during normal nursery sessions, taking care that children did not miss any favourite activities. Child Tracking, child observation and adult observations were also carried out by the EEL Support Worker during the agreed period. As the work progressed, some of the nursery staff offered to undertake observations of one or two children. They managed some Child Tracking observations but no others. In fact, they found this difficult as they needed to become familiar with the method of observation and had to maintain all their normal duties, and time to facilitate this staff development was hard to find. During this period some staff were absent and so were not able to help.

All adults working with the 2 to 5 year olds were happy for the EEL Support Worker to observe them working with children and carrying out the routines of the nursery as they did not have time to observe each other. The normal organisation and day-to-day management of the nursery was also carefully observed and documented. During this period, regular meetings were arranged with the head and the playroom leader to review progress and discuss concerns, or the project in general. It was not possible to hold regular meetings with all the playroom staff together as the shift system and their work and home commitments did not permit such arrangements. However, there were plenty of opportunities to talk in small groups for 10 to 20 minutes at coffee and lunch times. In this way, everyone was kept up to date with events, but deeper discussion with the team as a whole was not possible during this period. The EEL Support Worker made time to listen to all the playroom staff's views and concerns, whether they were linked to the Project or not. Achievements were noted and time was taken to talk with parents, children and staff and join in activities as much as possible. Contact was maintained with the babyroom staff as they too were interested in the Project.

The provision of time for staff discussion and training had already been identified by the head as a difficulty in developing practice in the nursery. The Management Committee were not able to provide extra staff to enable staff to have more time for discussion and training. During the last two years they had not been willing to close the nursery for a day or half-day for staff training.

EVALUATING PRACTICE

The evidence collected during the Evaluation Stage was put together and analysed by the EEL Support Worker, and given back to the nursery staff for discussion and reflection. There were some significant issues raised in the evaluation which the staff felt they needed to consider carefully. Some of the evidence was very reaffirming, whilst other evidence revealed aspects of their provision which required further thought and action.

The interviews with the head and staff showed that they all shared the view that the nursery should ensure that the children were happy and well cared for and that their needs were met within a safe learning environment. All agreed that policy was formulated by talk, writing and discussion between the head, Management Committee and staff. The head and playroom leader agreed that children should experience the full range of the curriculum, including intellectual, social and physical opportunities for children's learning. They stated that perhaps fewer mathematical and scientific activities were offered than was desirable but they hoped to develop this work. Other staff considered that the curriculum offered play experiences and learning and all agreed that staff planning meetings were important in ensuring continuity and progression.

Parents felt that there was sufficient communication. All parents agreed that the aims, objectives and practice of the nursery were shared as much as possible by talk and discussion, by notices, newsletters, meetings, individual contacts and by there being a very open, welcoming atmosphere in the nursery. They appreciated the opportunities their children had to learn and to play and were confident in the ability of the staff to meet their children's needs. The children who were interviewed discussed a variety of indoor and outdoor activities which they enjoyed, most of which were activities which allowed for child initiative. Favourites included playing with dolls, climbing, drawing, painting and using the computer. Their dislikes included 'noisy times', 'sitting down', 'listening when it is not a story' and 'waiting for people'.

The observation of children's Involvement showed that on a scale of 1 to 5, children achieved an average of 3.35 and were most involved when they were:

- engaged in imaginative play with other children in the home corner, den or outdoors;

- when they were involved in cooperative play with others, such as construction or small world activities;

- in freely chosen drawing or painting;

- in exploratory activities involving maths or science activities;

- in grouptimes when there was appropriate adult input, for example story or singing.

There was low Involvement when children were solitary, particularly outside, when they were asked to complete directed art or craft, or when the activities available offered little challenge. There were also periods of low Involvement when children were tired or waiting for the next happening, such as mealtimes, clearing up, storytime. The observations showed a need for more quiet time and rest, for the book corner to be regularly available, for more construction material and for more challenging activities for the mature, able children, both indoors and outside. Some activities, including painting, colouring, junk modelling, clay or dough, were not readily available during all sessions, and some maths or science activities, which could extend the older or more able children, were also often lacking. It was agreed that more time was needed for adults to join children's self-chosen activities so they could help to develop and extend the work. Observations showed that sometimes children did not have an opportunity to talk with an adult during a whole session. When an adult did sit down at an activity, she was soon surrounded by children eager to talk.

The evaluation revealed that the relatively short sessions of 1.25 hours in the morning and 1 hour in the afternoon were the only opportunities the children had to become deeply involved in their indoor activities. The constraints of tidying up indoors, getting ready for milk, lunch and tea, as well as setting up and clearing away outdoor equipment, meant staff gave considerable time to these tasks and much less time to listening and talking with the children or joining their activities. Lunchtime effectively took 2 hours, from 11.30 to 1.30, before activities resumed, and during this time it was difficult for tired children to rest.

The observation of the adults in the nursery showed that they were generally warm and supportive in their relationships with the children. However, there was limited time for adults to talk with, or listen to, individuals and small groups of children, due to the organisation in the nursery. Sometimes adults took opportunities to extend children's learning by explaining what was happening, for example the method of cleaning the fish tank, discussing the programme for the day or exploring the reason for the Lego building collapsing. At other times, there was far less adult stimulation, and some children had little experience of extended talk with an adult during several sessions. The observations demonstrated that children were generally well cared for by the staff. They were spoken to quietly, praised for their achievements, given positive feedback and reasons for decisions, and plenty of hugs when it seemed appropriate. Good table manners were encouraged and the serving of milk, lunch and tea were carefully organised. Some children found the prolonged sitting at tables and waiting difficult. Children were encouraged to be independent and serve and clear up themselves. In the playroom such

When an adult joined an activity she was soon surrounded by children eager to talk

independent skills were less in evidence and the adults put out and cleared away many materials, though children were encouraged to help.

Although the staff wanted to create a home from home, there was little opportunity for quiet rest for children. Children lay close together in the playroom after lunch to rest. Some managed to sleep and were stepped over carefully by those who couldn't. The evidence revealed that there was insufficient quiet space and opportunity for sleep for those who needed it. It also showed that the adults had a demanding task in educating and caring for the children in a confined space for many hours each day, with limited resources at their disposal. They were warm and caring in their attitudes and keen to increase the children's learning opportunities and refine their own skills, but the context often did not support them in their intentions.

ACTION PLANNING

The interviews, observations of children and adults, and general information about the nursery were documented in an Evaluation Report by the EEL

Support Worker. The participants agreed that this Report provided an accurate picture of the nursery. Several meetings were held to discuss the Evaluation and to develop an Action Plan to address some of the issues raised.

Before the Evaluation Report was presented to the staff, the head had already made some changes to the nursery routine. It was decided that children should have milk informally during the morning so that activities could stay out an extra half-hour until 10.15. Following the discussion of the Evaluation Report, the head and staff decided that the Action Plan should be viewed in three phases, a short-term period of one to two months, a medium period of three to six months and a long-term period of six months to a year or more. All the staff had contributed to the discussion and agreed with the plan and accepted the responsibilities it entailed. Working time was allocated for some of the planned tasks. The Action Plan had the following initiatives:

Short-term goals

- Making sure all children had everyday access to key experiences, including the book corner, drawing and colouring, free painting with a range of colours, maths activities, including measuring, time, large indoor bricks and construction materials;

- Increasing materials to extend maths and science activities in sand and water;

- Ensuring all children could rest if they wished to do so;

- Planning for staff training and development;

- Sharing the Evaluation Report and Action Plan with the Management Committee to enlist their interest and support.

All staff were asked by the head to contribute to the implementation of these changes and to agree individual responsibilities. Nursery nurses and other staff agreed to ensure that a wider range of materials was available for children. Purchase of new material was planned by the head, who also arranged a Saturday in-service day on early science and maths provided by an LEA Adviser. The plans were discussed with the Management Committee.

Medium-term goals

- Purchase of more reference books showing work situations, people and landscapes in Britain and overseas;

- Increasing the range of multicultural materials;

- Increasing the materials for shop, hospital and office play;

- Developing the use of children's own interests as starting points for their activities and developing strategies for sensitive intervention which will lead to their deeper involvement.

The head arranged to purchase more books and it was agreed to ask parents to help provide more materials for multicultural education and for role-play purposes. It was felt that staff training would help them to use more effectively children's interests as starting points for learning.

Long-term goals

- Developing the system of monitoring and recording children's development with a key worker system;

- Increasing the number of walks and visits;

- Increasing the range of adults to talk to and share a skill with children.

It was agreed to ask parents to accompany children on walks and visits and share skills with them. The head planned to introduce a key worker system.

It was recognised that the goals were ambitious but the head and staff wished to address the main issues raised in the Evaluation Report in order to develop the quality of children's care and education in the nursery.

IMPROVING PRACTICE

The nursery team began implementing the Action Plan and were supported by the Management Committee, who allocated money for equipment and to enable staff to make training visits and to attend courses. The short-term actions were begun immediately, and nursery staff could see the benefit of the reorganisation of milk time. They also enjoyed using the new books, science and maths materials with the children. Making sure that all children had regular access to the range of curriculum experiences proved more difficult. Outdoor times and meals were unaltered so the children still only had 1.50 hours in the morning and 1 hour in the afternoon in which to pursue their chosen activities indoors. Progress was slow and sometimes uncertain but gradually the changes could be seen. The in-service training day helped to develop the work. Staff visits to

Children cooperated well together, shared and took turns with material

other nurseries focused on curriculum and organisation, and discussion at staff meetings helped them to reflect on their own practice. The increased contact with other early years workers helped staff to develop practice in the nursery and provide a wider range of experience for the children.

Financial constraints limited the purchase of more reference books, the provision of large wooden bricks and more complex construction materials for older children. Parents and staff were unable to increase provision of role-play and multicultural materials, though they were still recognised as important. Progress on these medium-term goals was thus limited by lack of time and funding for the busy adults involved. However, the staff increasingly were using children's interests as starting points for learning, and developing strategies of sensitive intervention, with the intention of increasing children's deeper involvement.

The longer-term goal of developing a key worker system was started and staff all liked having greater opportunities to relate to a particular group of children and their parents. A new system of record keeping was introduced by the head. Parents also signed a general permission slip, enabling their child to go on local visits and walks. However, in practice these have rarely been arranged due to lack of staff availability and confidence. Parents and others were invited to share a skill with children. The one or two who responded were well received and it was hoped that this would continue to grow.

The head and staff were pleased with the outcome of their initiatives, particularly the introduction of staff training, the key worker system and changes in the nursery curriculum and organisation. They regretted that lack of funds and parent support had limited the provision of new resources but hoped that this would be overcome in the longer term by planned fundraising. They expressed great satisfaction with the progress achieved in many of the areas they identified, despite the difficult financial circumstances.

REFLECTION ON ACTION

The parents and the Management Committee supported the changes embarked upon in the nursery. Increasingly they recognised that maintaining quality care and education for their children required the provision of increased equipment and resources to stimulate children's learning, together with access to training for staff to update their skills and to provide motivation and feedback. Parents were so happy with the nursery provision, the warm caring attitudes of the staff and the education provided in the extended hours, that it was sometimes difficult for some of them to understand that their children needed access to a broader range of experience, and that staff needed opportunities for increased training and time for meetings and reflection about their work.

The children continued to enjoy their time in the nursery. Sometimes they had a wider range of activities available and increased opportunities to develop their own ideas in creative work as a result of the organisational changes. They enjoyed using the new books and equipment which helped them to extend their play and learning. They appreciated adults talking with them more regularly and enjoyed taking milk informally. The average level of children's Involvement increased from 3.35 level to 3.82 during the period of the EEL Project. This clearly demonstrated that children were more deeply immersed in their activities and were less easily distracted, experiencing more intense moments of concentration.

The staff cooperated well in developing the changes they had agreed upon. They appreciated the support given by the Management Committee to purchase some equipment and to enable them to participate in training and visits. They were pleased with the changes in the morning organisation and spent more time listening to, and talking with, children. This was also reflected in the Adult

Engagement Scale results, which showed adults listening more to the children, being more responsive and stimulating them more effectively. They were also increasingly using children's interests as a starting point for learning.

The head and staff made a range of initiatives during the period of the EEL Project. Resources were improved and changes made in organisation, in curriculum and in opportunities for training. All of these were achieved against a background of financial constraint, changes in staff, limited support from busy parents and limited time available for full staff meetings and discussions. The achievements of the staff in a relatively short period were considerable and a foundation was laid for future development. The EEL Project proved a most valuable starting point for change, reflection and development in the nursery with benefits to the children, staff and parents.

ISSUES FOR FURTHER REFLECTION

This Case Study describes how a team of private day nursery workers opened up their provision to a process of systematic evaluation and improvement. They worked intensively with an EEL Support Worker and developed an Action Plan to:

- modify their nursery routines

- broaden the children's learning opportunities

- introduce a key worker system.

The processes they went through in achieving this improvement in their practice raise a number of important questions for discussion by those who work both within this type of setting and beyond.

1   What are the benefits and difficulties in catering for children from 0 to 5 years in one setting? Should there be more mixed aged grouping or single aged grouping, and for what kind of activity?

2   Is it possible for practitioners to carry out this kind of evaluation themselves? Can an outsider make appropriate assessments? What are the difficulties facing practitioners who want to carry out observations and other evaluative procedures?

3   How might private day nurseries build in time for staff development?

4   What do you feel were the factors which influenced the children's level of Involvement in this setting? How might they have been raised?

5   How important are routines for staff and children? What should the balance be between routine and free flow?

6   How important are quiet areas for young children in all day care? How do we create these in a busy nursery?

7   What are the key learning experiences which should be available to young children?

8   What are the benefits of a key worker system? Should all young children have them?

4 Case Study Four – A Pre-school Playgroup

Fiona Ramsden

Context

This playgroup was situated in a parish church hall in close proximity to the church and its small community in a city suburb. The playgroup was a member of the Pre-school Learning Alliance, which provided support and organised staff training courses if required. There were thirty-four children on roll. The playgroup was legally allowed twenty-four children per session and all places were usually filled. It was open in the morning from 9.20–12.05 on Mondays, Wednesdays, Thursdays and Fridays. The children's ages ranged from 2 to 4 years of age. At the time of the Project there were 5 children aged 2+ years, 17 children aged 3 years, and 12 children aged 4 years. The playgroup catchment area was very local. There were no children from one-parent families, or whose parents first language was not English or were from an ethnic minority. There were two children whom the playgroup leader identified as experiencing difficulties with learning. The playgroup was supervised by the leader who had taken up the position two years previously, with two children of her own attending the group at that time. She led a team of eight staff.

The playgroup was completely self-financing. Fees of £1.80 per child per session paid for staff wages and the hire of the hall and, as the letter to new parents stated,

> We are a non-profit making organisation and we have to rely on parents raising the money themselves for everything else – from painting, cooking, model-making and buying toys to summer outings and Christmas parties. We always need help, ideas and money.

The playgroup was organised by the leader and her staff along with a Management Committee. Members were voted onto the Committee which comprised a voluntary group of parents. Its function was to care for the administration, finance and fundraising of the playgroup. It met at least once per term. The committee was used as a means of sounding out new ideas from its members and the staff. It tried to support any new policies or ventures in which the staff wished to participate and vice-versa. For example, when the leader and staff needed new equipment, including toys and books, the Committee agreed to try to raise the necessary funds. Similarly on another occasion Committee members needed to urgently raise capital to pay for increased hall rental, and the staff agreed to a pay cut. Policy was formulated in joint collaboration between the leader, the staff, and the Committee. The aim of the playgroup was clearly stated in the introductory letter to new parents:

> *Welcome to this Community Playgroup – Your Playgroup. We hope your children will enjoy themselves with us, gain confidence and acquire some of the many skills needed to enjoy a happy and fulfilled life.*

The staff who were interviewed had very similar feelings with regard to the aims of playgroup. They stressed that their main role was to stimulate the children. The leader felt that preparation for school was a 'side issue' and that their main aim at playgroup was to help children to 'learn through play'. Similarly another staff member felt the purpose of playgroup was,

> *to give the opportunity for children to play in a safe and stimulating environment, where they could learn social skills and about their environment.*

The importance of the children feeling 'welcome', 'secure' and 'loved' was stressed by one staff member, along with specific learning aims such as:

> *to encourage their speech, confidence, finger manipulation and group experiences not received at home.*

The children interviewed were rather unsure about why they came to playgroup, but as one child stated, 'I come to playgroup because I like it' and another said 'I like coming that's why!'

Physical environment and facilities

The environment consisted of one large hall (see Figure 4.1) which had large windows to floor level on both sides, but the impression was still one of a dark space. One member of staff summed up the staff's feelings about the hall:

> *The hall is very depressing – we always have to have the light on, even in the summer. It badly needs decorating – the ceiling has grey panels which could be whitened.*

Wood shavings in a water trough

In the hall there were four or five low child-sized tables with chairs, on which games, puzzles and creative art work were placed. Near to the kitchen the home corner or shop, sand, wood shavings and painting easels or water play were situated and were rotated on a daily basis.

At the far end of the room there was an area set aside for floor play on a mat or the climbing frame. As the leader suggested,

> *It is a large area for the children to play with bigger construction toys, and this end is then used for storytime away from the noise from clearing away in the kitchen and cupboard.*

Set in one of the windows was the book corner, which had a piece of carpet on the floor, a bean bag, two child-size chairs and a wide wooden ledge for children to sit and look at books. There was a selection of pushchairs and dressing-up clothes available for the children, but wheeled bikes and vehicles were not allowed because of the lack of storage space. Generally, the equipment, toys and facilities were in excellent condition. This was largely due to the care and attention given to them by the staff. The toys and equipment available was varied and they suited the age and development of all the children. As the leader stated there was a:

> *good variety with different uses and settings. The farm animals can go in the farm, in the playdough and be used with the building blocks.*

New equipment was bought and acquired when funds allowed. The shop was built by a playgroup child's father and was a huge success with the children. There was much use of available resources in true playgroup tradition: paper towel rolls, old computer paper, old deodorant bottles (washed!) used for painting and old cardboard boxes for junk modelling. Unfortunately, much to the staff's annoyance, the playgroup was not allowed to place anything on the walls of the hall as it was used by many other community groups. However, unofficially the internal wall nearest to the kitchen was used to display some of the children's artwork. Each term, a large seasonal mural depicting the playgroup children's work was displayed in the church. The children found it very exciting when they took their mural in procession to the church and invited their parents to go to look at it. One adult-sized table was kept to one side of the hall to display the theme for the week. The children did bring their own belongings, such as a well-loved toy or blanket, to playgroup.

There were adequate toilet and kitchen facilities for the playgroup. There was a walk-in cupboard situated inside the kitchen where all the playgroup equipment had to be stored each day. This restricted the resources available at playgroup but the staff had become very adept at stacking the cupboard and making the most of it. However, one member summed up the staff's feelings:

> *The cupboard is a major problem . . . accidents happen, fingers get trapped and toys fall out of the boxes stacked on the top shelf. Almost a hard hat area!*

On the opposite side of the hall there was access to the outside area. This was an open grassed piece of land, formerly the graveyard to the church. Playgroup staff fenced off the outside area temporarily when needed. This grassed area was used if the weather was fine in the summer. Balls, hoops, bean bags and water and sand play were taken outside for the children to play with. The children were always supervised outside and indeed it was usually a grouptime activity.

The participants' views on the physical environment were similar in many ways. They all recognised that the playgroup staff did the best they could given the circumstances. The parents seemed very happy with the environment of the playgroup. As one parent stated,

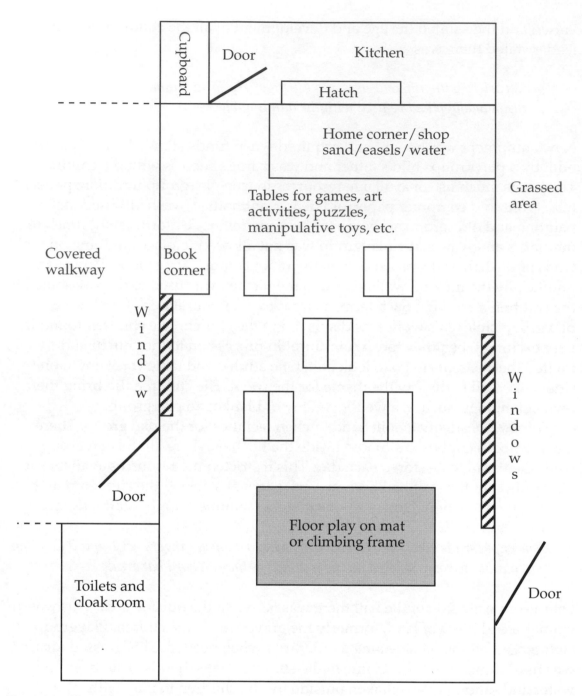

Figure 4.1   Plan of the playgroup hall

I'm happy with the physical environment of the playgroup, it's the best given the facilities and money they have.

However, she felt that,

If there was more money from the Government then there could be more space, separate rooms for quiet and busy activities – but this is not a criticism of the playgroup!

Another parent felt the playgroup was, 'A pleasant environment being light and airy' but that 'more display on the walls of what the children have done' was needed.

The staff had a long list of improvements they would like for the playgroup. These included more space for the children 'to let off steam', 'more room for wheeled bikes, trikes, physical exercise', 'another room would be great', 'I'd like a corner! – a real book corner – a separate place for quiet or loud individual time', 'funding does not allow us to have soft play but neither does the space available'. Most of the staff felt there was a great advantage to having the grassed area outside made available to the playgroup. However, the leader felt,

I'd like an outdoor area for when it's wet and particularly as the grass gets so wet.

It was clear that the children enjoyed going outside to the grassed area, as they were very quick to inform the staff if the weather was fine. Certain activities, such as the pushchairs and dressing-up, proved to be popular so the staff tended to put them out more regularly. The shop and climbing frame caused great excitement with the children also.

Staffing

The playgroup was staffed with a leader who was NNEB and PLA trained and held a first aid qualification. She had experience with children as a nanny, crèche worker, childminder and mother. She led a staff of eight colleagues, all of whom held the PLA basic course. The playgroup relied on extra help from volunteer parents. There were four members of staff present at each session with one volunteer helper if available. It was clear from their professional biographies that many of the staff at the playgroup saw their role as 'a friend to the children', 'to provide a wide variety of skills for the children and opportunities not always available at home', 'to help the children overcome fears and increase their own sense of worth' and, as one member of staff described,

I feel my role is that of an aunty, ensuring that the children feel happy, secure and confident in my care, both in group activities and as individuals, always giving a sympathetic ear.

Some staff members saw their role more as a 'bridge between mother and school'. However, another group of staff saw their role as providing 'good quality play opportunities', seeing themselves as being more 'objective than if they were in the parent role'. As one member of staff noted,

We allow a child to go to his limits rather than being curtailed.

The parents felt the staff provided a variety of roles. One parent commented,

There are different varieties of helper – the mum, the teacher, the grandma – it's like home so children can relate to them.

The parents recognised that it was important for their children to have these differing staff roles. At times the children needed 'to show respect' and 'discipline' but at playgroup there should be an 'opportunity for a cuddle too'. The children saw the staff's role as 'to look after the children' and that they come to playgroup 'to do some work'. One child recognised that the adults 'show me how to play with things'. The staff worked very much as a team with everyone helping each other with regard to all the tasks at playgroup. The playgroup leader organised the day-to-day running of the playgroup by a staff rota system. One member of staff is deployed on the activity associated with the theme each morning and the rest of the staff follow the rota.

As a consequence of the new legislation, particularly the Children Act of 1989, the PLA has stated that all its staff members should hold at least the PLA Basic Course. The playgroup had actively tried to maintain this level of training for the staff. However, funds were difficult to raise and so this had been a lengthy procedure. The leader would also have liked some of the staff to complete a first aid course. She was keen to support any staff member 'who wants to further their knowledge', but she found financial difficulties limiting. There were two member of staff who noted on their professional biographies that they would like specific training, one in first aid and the other 'an intense training course covering all further aspects of childcare'.

STRATEGIES FOR WORKING TOGETHER

Initially the playgroup leader was approached by the EEL Support Worker, to ask if she would consider taking part in the Project. The playgroup leader was very interested by the sound of the EEL Quality Evaluation and Development Process and asked if the staff and the Support Worker could meet together to discuss it further. An evening meeting was agreed and the whole process was discussed at length with the staff of the playgroup. There were two main questions raised at the meeting.

- The staff were keen for the parents to be involved as much as possible.

- The staff wanted to know for what purpose the information from the playgroup would be used.

The EEL process already ensured that parents were very involved. The procedures ensuring anonymity and confidentiality, advocated by the EEL Project, were accepted and they were assured that they would be kept informed of any developments at all times.

Once all the questions had been answered, everyone seemed very keen to start. One staff member stated, 'It'll make us pull our socks up!' and to the Support Worker's question of when would they like to start, came the answer 'tomorrow'. The Committee were informed of the Project at an evening meeting, and they were pleased to be involved. They suggested that a notice be placed on the board in the entrance to the playgroup informing parents of the Project and asking for any queries or further information to be directed towards the playgroup leader, who would then contact the Support Worker. There were no queries from the parents but each time a parent came in to help at a playgroup session the Support Worker talked to him or her about the Project and what was to be achieved.

Although a large proportion of the information was collected by the EEL Support Worker, the staff were shown the data at every stage and there was discussion about what had been seen and recorded that session. Often, with a little gentle persuasion, a member of staff would carry out an Involvement observation in the playgroup. On one occasion Mrs C. observed Andrea in the garden along with all of the playgroup children:

> Andrea was pretending to be a soldier with two other children. She had a stick held across her like a rifle. They were all marching up and down the garden, totally oblivious of the other children's ball game. Mrs B. (a staff member) told Andrea to put down the stick as it was dangerous, and then walked over to her and further explained that the stick must be put down. Andrea looked surprised, stared at the retreating staff member and then carried on pretending to be a soldier without a stick!

Mrs C. was fascinated to observe that, despite the interruption of the activity, Andrea remained deeply involved in her play. She recognised the importance of adults being alert to individual children's needs and the power of observation. Obviously, the observing member of staff had felt the stick would be dangerous to Andrea, yet, in this case, this was not true. Often adults do need to react quickly in situations where children's safety is at risk. However, this scenario raised the important issue of power and control, as Riley (1984, p.53) suggested:

> *When we attempt to direct children's play we are violating rights that are unquestionably theirs. Adults too often intrude into the world of the playing child with advice and ideas, robbing the child of freedom to grow and learn through his natural medium.*

This incident showed how important it is for the practitioners to carry out at least some of the data collection themselves. Gradually all the staff and some parent helpers took part in the collection of the data. The sharing of the observations helped to build up a collaborative working relationship within the playgroup. Similarly the Support Worker built up the trust of the playgroup practitioners by being prepared to help out when they needed. At the end of the session she would help to clean up or if there was a staff shortage she would work with the children.

EVALUATING PRACTICE

The practitioners and the Support Worker together began to build up a picture of the playgroup. This culminated in the writing of the Evaluation Report which consisted of a resumé of all the documents, observations, and interviews collected together. It used the EEL 10 dimensions of quality as a framework and took into account the views of all the participants in the setting – the children, the parents, the staff and the playgroup leader. The draft Report was read by all the staff and on the whole they said they found it 'very useful' in providing a basis from which they could evaluate their own practice and plan for development. The Evaluation Report was then altered to ensure that it provided a fair and valid picture of practice for all the participants in the setting.

At this stage it was very important that the practitioners felt able to celebrate the areas of their practice that worked well, even though there was a human tendency to look at all the aspects that they did not feel happy with. It was at this point that the Support Worker's role was to encourage the practitioners and help them to celebrate their successes because the Evaluation Report had illuminated many very positive aspects of the playgroup's practice. The playgroup clearly could celebrate a number of areas of their practice and this provides a positive foundation from which to develop.

Learning and teaching styles

The aim of all the participants in the playgroup was for the children's learning to be provided through play. As one staff member noted 'play is marvellous – it does not need to be in the form of expensive toys, for example sand gives wonderful imaginative play', and 'we supply the play materials and the imagination of the children takes off'. The staff felt that having established the play environment it was their role to 'give praise for effort', 'guidance', 'encouragement' and 'to maintain a balance where sometimes the adults need to take the lead from the children, and at others the children need to be stimulated'. One indication of the children's learning is their level of involvement, as assessed with the Child Involvement Scale. This scale is based on the idea that a child is more likely to be learning if she shows signals of high involvement, for example concentration, persistence, creativity and precision. The observations had demonstrated the level of Involvement experienced at the playgroup during the study period.

It was clear that at playgroup there was a high incidence of level 5 (high Involvement) with 25 per cent of the occurrences being at this level. The average level of Involvement for the playgroup was 3.22.

Relationships and interaction

One of the main aims of the playgroup was for the staff to provide 'a loving, caring and secure' relationship with the children. Another aim was to help the children 'to learn independence but with adults that also give them security'. Great importance was placed on 'being seen to be fair' with all the children. The interviews with the parents showed that they felt very happy with the relationships and interaction within the playgroup. As one mother stated, 'they definitely get it all here – if they didn't, I wouldn't send him.' Another parent felt that the staff acted as a team which evolved by 'picking the right adults'.

The Adult Engagement Scale and the Target Child observation instruments showed that the playgroup's aims were supported in practice. The adult data indicate that the staff show high levels of Sensitivity towards the children, particularly in relation to their performance. There are also high levels of Stimulation in the form of the adults' positive role in child-initiated communication and in giving input. The importance of positive adult interaction is indicated in a scenario observed at playgroup:

Kathy is sticking tissue paper onto a balloon. There are three children and one adult on the table. Kathy is asked by the adult how she is feeling because she has recently had a hospital visit. Kathy replied 'I've been poorly but I'm better now.' *She explains to the adult about the hospital and that she had to sleep in a cot. Kathy was quite concerned about this:* 'I'm not a baby, anymore!' *The adult then took the opportunity to explain to her about the beds in hospitals and to chat about all the questions that Kathy had.*

The Target Child observations captured the type and number of interactions between 10 target children and their peers/adults. It was clear from this analysis that 65 per cent of interactions were initiated by the target children and 35 per cent were non-initiated. The tone of the talk was also analysed and indicated that most (94 per cent) of the talk was very positive in nature. The following is an example of positive interaction between the children.

It is pack-away time. Steve (a child) *packs away various toys whilst talking to a group of children. Then he picks up some cars from the floor and packs them away in a large container. An argument ensues between another boy and Steve over who should carry the container to the cupboard. It is pulled between them for several minutes until the two children decide mutually to* 'Let's carry it together!' *The argument changes to excitement and lots of giggles as they try to hold the container together.*

Parental partnership

The staff recognised the importance of parental partnership, and this was noted by one staff member:

The biggest influence on the child is the parent. We're a first stage, a step away from the parents, so we need to liaise with them. We do it – we are receptive . . .

The playgroup did liaise actively with parents through the termly newsletter which outlined forthcoming events and fundraising, a welcoming notice board and a parent helper system. These mechanisms led to communication which allowed parents 'to see what's happening and so feel involved'. The staff were always readily available at the beginning and end of the session to talk with parents. Parents, staff and children had the opportunity to meet at fundraising events such as coffee mornings. All of the children interviewed enjoyed their parents coming in to help: it was regarded by many as being a very special occasion. As one child stated, 'yes I like mummy coming to help – I give out the biscuits.'

ACTION PLANNING

As soon as the practitioners had started on the Evaluation and Development process they had begun to think about their practice. However it was at an Action Planning meeting held one evening with all the staff present, that many issues and concerns were raised as a result of the Evaluation Report. It was important at this point that the staff did not take on too much all at once and so certain aspects were outlined which were felt by the staff to be worthy of development.

1   The individual child observations indicated to the staff that they all needed to spend time observing the children.
2   As a consequence of a combination of the results of the Child Tracking data, the Adult Engagement observations and the interviews, the staff decided that they wanted to provide the children with more Autonomy. The individual Child Tracking data indicated that within the Zone of Initiative, or level of free choice, the children had only a limited amount of choice in their own selection of activity. The children were most often guided by the activities that were placed out for them by the staff.

CHILD TRACKING DATA: ZONE OF INITIATIVE

Level	Description of level	No. of incidence
Level 1	No choice for the child	15
Level 2	Limited choices	25
Level 3	Some activities are excluded	–
Level 4	Child has freedom of choice	–

The Adult Engagement observations revealed that staff showed high levels of Sensitivity and Stimulation, in the form of encouraging child-initiated communication and in giving input to an activity. However, generally there were fewer observed incidents of children's Autonomy being supported, particularly in the correction of children's behaviour, in the staff's provision for the children's own ideas and their judgment of the end product. It was clear that the children see the staff as the enforcers of discipline. One child stated, 'Hilda *(staff)* tells me what I can and can't do.'

3   As a result of the Child Tracking data the staff decided that they wanted to ensure all areas of the curriculum were well provided. It is difficult in any early years setting to define exactly what children are learning. They can often experience a wide range and variety of activities at any one time. For example, a water trough can provide science, mathematics, role-play and creative, social and language experiences for a young child. The Child Tracking data provided an indication, during the observation period, of how often the various curriculum areas were covered at the nursery. This data showed the most frequent curriculum areas covered were social/moral, language/literacy, and aesthetic/creative. The playgroup did not possess a computer so obviously this was an area that was not covered. Areas not so frequently experienced were physical, maths and science.

Improving Practice

Having decided on the areas that they wanted to improve, the playgroup staff wrote an Action Plan which set out their aims, objectives and strategies. The Plan explained who would be responsible for each small part of the action and supplied a timescale. Once the Action Plan was agreed by all the staff, then each member was provided with her own copy. This enabled all the participants to feel they had a part to play in the action. The action that was planned was quite wide-ranging.

Training in observation techniques

The first strategy was to provide all the staff with in-service Involvement training. Once trained, the Support Worker relieved the staff, one at a time, of their duties so that they could carry out observations of individual children. Through these observations the staff realised that:

• The period after breaktime had particularly low levels in the children's Involvement, so they decided to experiment with different activities at this time. Each member of staff led a small group of children in an associated activity, for example jigsaws, a board game, puzzles or a theme such as colours. This gave the children an opportunity to be involved at a higher level, to participate in a small group and to interact with an adult.

- Previously the blockplay, construction and train set were situated on the floor on a large mat and were virtually ignored by the children and the adults. Very rarely did the adults interact with the children in these activities – they tended to concentrate on the craft activities on the tables instead. As an experiment the blockplay, construction and train set were placed upon tables to ease access for both the children and the adults. The adults began to take an active interest in these areas. This change indicated to the children that all activities were equally important, and encouraged the play interaction between the adults and the children.

Increasing Autonomy

The staff wanted to provide the children with more Autonomy. The staff and the Support Worker had long discussions on how to approach this important area. The staff had already taken the first steps by observing the children so that they knew when a child needed help and when it was best to stand back. One staff member wanted to do everything for the children, out of kindness. As she stated, 'The hardest part of this is standing back and not completing the activity for them', and yet as the Project continued and we talked about her observations, she began to realise that children needed to do things for themselves and that in this way they learn. As she stated later in her feedback on the process, 'The project helped me to see that standing back and watching is just as important as helping and taking over.'

The Adult Engagement data summarised these positive changes that took place in the playgroup. The data was collected again after the Development phase and revealed significant improvements. It was clear that the staff were still extremely sensitive to the children. In addition, there was an increase in their Sensitivity to the children's performance, giving lots of positive praise and responding to the children's needs readily. In the area of Stimulation, there was a definite improvement in their ability to encourage children's activity and dialogue appropriately. The staff were more open to different approaches introduced by the children and were allowing the children to experiment, rather than having an adult's predetermined aim to the final outcome. The aspect of adult Autonomy showed the greatest positive change, with the staff giving much more provision for the children's experimentation, ideas and choice of interests.

Before the experiment

During the experiment

An Action Plan experiment – construction activities were placed on tables and adults provided stimulation when and where necessary

REFLECTION ON ACTION

One of the major problems that the playgroup had to face daily was associated with funding. The staff needed to have access to non-contact time so they could plan and discuss playgroup sessions. The EEL Quality Evaluation and Development process highlighted this issue, as it was very difficult to arrange meetings and interviews to discuss the Project because the staff often had other jobs to help support the meagre wage paid to them from the playgroup. Time to talk had to be snatched during lunchtime or in the evening before staff left for other work. The meetings that were held were always unpaid for the staff.

All of the playgroup practitioners savoured the opportunity that the Project provided for them to observe individual children. They began to recognise the importance of observation in its own right. As one staff member stated, 'I like taking time to watch the children's involvement in what they are doing.' The playgroup leader was keen to 'encourage staff to continue to repeatedly sit back and watch' the children. Some of the staff wanted access to more training and as one stated, 'it made me realise that to really make full use of the project I need to go back to school . . .'

One of the main purposes of the Quality Evaluation and Development Process was for the action to have a positive impact upon practice and practitioners and, ultimately, on the effective learning of young children. One method of recording this effectiveness is through an analysis of the children's levels of Involvement. It was clear at the end of the process that the children were experiencing higher levels of Involvement in the playgroup than when compared with the beginning of the process. There was a definite increase of level 5 (high) Involvement from 25 per cent previously, to 39 per cent. Fewer children were experiencing level 1 (low) Involvement. The average Involvement level had increased noticeably from 3.22 to 3.94. This substantial increase provided the staff with hard evidence of the impact of their action on improving the quality of learning they were able to offer the children.

ISSUES FOR FURTHER REFLECTION

This Case Study describes how a team of playgroup workers collaborated with an EEL Support Worker to look systematically at the quality of their provision and to develop an Action Plan for improvement. The focus of their action was:

- developing their observation skills
- giving the children more choice and autonomy.

The processes they went through in achieving this improvement in their practice raise a number of important questions for discussion by those who work both within this type of setting and beyond.

1   What are the challenges in providing a stimulating environment in a multipurpose large hall? How might this be achieved?
2   The importance of time for staff development was clear in this playgroup. How might they have allocated time for this?
3   The EEL Support Worker stressed the importance of developing her relationship with the playgroup workers. What strategies did she use?
4   The importance of celebrating success as well as highlighting areas of development was notable in this Case Study. What did they celebrate and identify for development? Do you agree with their priorities?
5   What are the difficulties in finding time for observing children? How valuable do you think this is?
6   What are the issues raised by observing adults interacting with children? Who might carry out these observations?
7   Do you agree that children need to be given Autonomy? Could this playgroup have further increased Autonomy?
8   How far do you feel Involvement is a good measure of the quality of children's learning? What do you think were the factors which led to an increase in this setting?

5 CASE STUDY FIVE – A SOCIAL SERVICES DAY NURSERY

Maureen Saunders

CONTEXT

In 1974 the religious group, The Society of Friends, approached the local Social Services and offered their buildings as a nursery for priority children who had been referred by health visitors and Social Services. The buildings were situated in a designated new town area which housed relocated inner-city families. The nursery opened in 1974 as a traditional day nursery providing day care for small groups of children, with two or three members of staff. The day nursery was located close to flats built for one-parent families, and initially it took the children only from these flats. However, as the new town developed so priorities changed, and gradually the 24-child day nursery grew and began to work with some forty families. The name also changed to become a Family Resource Centre, in order to better reflect the work being undertaken. It functioned as a specialist resource offering support to under-5s and their families, and a range of facilities to meet individual needs. Children were taken from all over the large town, but attendance continued to be through referral, with the majority of children having some developmental delay.

When the EEL Project was undertaken, a large proportion of the children's parents were unemployed, and none came from professional groups. All the children spoke English as a first language and most experienced difficulties in social behaviour; ten children were from one-parent families and two were from ethnic minority groups. An assessment was made for the payment of fees but, as all families were from a low income group and came under what is called a 'nil assessment', no fees were charged for food or care for the children at the Centre.

The Centre provided care from 9 am until 4 pm for children from 18 months to 5 years. At the time of the Project, the day care sessions from Monday to Thursday catered for twenty children. Individual children were given places on a two to four day basis, according to need. Within this group there were fifteen 3 and 4 year olds, each of whom attended on all of the four days. Sessional opportunities were also available for other children with specific needs, providing support such as speech and behavioural therapy. Totstime was also held on Monday and Thursday mornings from 9.30–12 noon for the under-3s. This was organised as a parenting group, with discussions on the needs of the parent and the child, and parents were committed to attend one of the two weekly sessions. Outreach visits were also made by staff to children and families in the local area.

From 1989–1990 a Social Services Working Party had reviewed the practice of the Centre and set the pattern of working procedures for the different sessions, i.e. Day Care, Totstime and Outreach. They had also defined the services offered within the Centre. Following this review, the staff at the Centre had looked at their policy and practice in some detail, but their written policy had not yet been completed.

Policy

The staff team were responsible for the day-to-day policy of the Centre. Their brochure explained that their overall aim was to:

> provide a safe, secure, stimulating environment where children have opportunities to play and express their feelings in a 1:1 situation or in larger group activities ... and to encourage parental involvement in their child's/children's care by giving support and help in managing their child/children.

More specifically the NNEB qualified staff team worked directly with the children in partnership with the parent or carer, both within the Centre and, in some cases, through the Outreach work in the home.

Staffing

The staff, who worked from 8.30 am–5 pm Monday to Thursday and from 9 am–4 pm on Fridays, included a Centre Manager, a Deputy Manager (two people shared this post), four full-time Nursery Officers, one part-time Nursery Assistant (13 hours), a Cook (25 hours), a part-time Kitchen Assistant and a part-time Clerical Worker. One further member of staff was seconded to take a Diploma in Social Work and this vacancy was used to create more nursery assistant hours and ten clerical hours. NNEB and Diploma in Social Work students were also trained at the Centre.

Each Deputy and Nursery Officer was a Key Worker for particular children or families. They helped to draw up the agreement between parents and the Centre about what the Centre and the parents planned to do to meet the needs of the child. The Key Workers were also responsible for record keeping, reviews and assessments of the children. The reviews were formal meetings, chaired by the Centre Manager, where each child's case was discussed by the parents and relevant staff. The staff also acted as co-workers for other children at the Centre, having to stand in if a member of staff left or was absent. The Key worker's role was one of counselling, advising and helping parents with strategies for managing their children.

Physical environment

The Family Resource Centre was well resourced with materials and apparatus for all aspects of learning, and was housed in the Quaker Meeting House, which had some built-in nursery facilities. Children's work was well displayed in all areas of the building (except in the round Meeting room), and these added colour and interest to a lively environment. The Friends' Meeting room was

Children working in the round meeting room. The furniture and equipment has to be carried in at the beginning of the session and cleared again by lunchtime

used, but restricted to non-messy play. However, sheets were sometimes spread on the floor so that painting or playdough activities could be catered for when the other rooms were being used for free play activities. Small carpets were put down for floor activities, but any furniture needed for the children had to be carried in from the other classroom and returned again for lunchtime. The soft play equipment was used and stored in this large room from Monday to Thursday, when it had to be removed for the weekend meetings of the Friends. This room was also used for Parents' Circle and reviews so was unavailable to children at those times.

The classroom had cupboards and open shelving, housing most of the Centre's resources. It had children's furniture and trays for their belongings, a sink, and adult work tables and chairs. It was used for all sand and water play, for Totstime activities on Monday and Thursday mornings, and as a dining room each day for children and adults. The room could be partitioned off to make two smaller rooms, and these were used for most afternoon small group sessions.

A small carpeted room was used for watching TV, for story, for pre-school activity sessions, as a staffroom, as a medical room when the doctor visited, for individual work with children and families, as an interview room, for staff

Children loved the thrill of travelling down this slope on a variety of wheeled toys

supervision and for further storage of books, videos, puzzles and for all Totstime equipment. The inner foyer housed the children's coat pegs, and books were displayed on a carpet square which was used for storytime or for gathering the children together.

The rear entrance of the building opened off the children's washroom with sinks, toilets and sluice. This often created a bottleneck, and gave no privacy to a child being bathed or changed. Leading off from this bathroom was a laundry which was shared with the tenants of the adjacent flats. A well-equipped kitchen was used to prepare hot lunches, light teas and drinks for children and staff.

The outside play area was small. It was well fenced but had a steeply sloping paved path and grassed area. A flat slabbed area was partially covered by an overhanging verandah. On this area was a wooden shed which housed the wheeled toys, bats, balls and other outside equipment. This equipment had to be packed and unpacked for each session. There was no fixed outside equipment.

STRATEGIES FOR WORKING TOGETHER

Initial contact was made with the Centre by the EEL Project Director to outline the aims and scope of the EEL Project. After further discussions between the Manager and Centre staff it was agreed that the Project should go ahead within the setting. The Deputy Director of the EEL Project and the EEL Support Worker attended a team meeting of all the staff at the Centre, when the process they would be undertaking was discussed and the implications of the EEL Project for them. The staff were very quiet during this meeting and asked very few questions. On reflection, the Support Worker felt at this stage they were a little overawed and unsure of how the project might affect them, and how they could take part. However, they agreed that if the project would help them to help the children they would be happy to participate.

The Support Worker kept her first visits to the setting short and very informal. She wanted to get a 'feel' for the place, and get the staff and children used to seeing her around. She did not start the more formal observations of children and adults which the Project requires until later. She concentrated on getting to know people, letting them get to know her, and encouraging them to see her as one of them, willing to assist in any way. At first everyone was a little apprehensive – understandably so, for here was an outsider coming into a setting and a well-established team to observe the staff and their children. The staff were very cheerful and outgoing and quickly accepted the Support Worker as one of their team, but it took longer for the children to respond to her, for most of them had some emotional difficulties and found forming relationships, especially with newcomers, very demanding. But eventually most got to know and trust her, and they would approach her and ask for help, talk or just smile.

As the Support Worker went about the business of collecting information for the Project everyone was extremely helpful, open and honest. They very willingly gave their valuable time to answering her many questions. She gave careful explanations and described how the information would be used to build up a picture of the setting. Although they were extremely interested in the Child Tracking observations, the Child Involvement observations and the Adult Engagement observations, at this point they could not be persuaded to have a go at the observations for themselves. They preferred to leave it to the Support Worker who had to respect their wishes. At this stage it was a case of slowly building up a relationship of trust, and developing the confidence of the staff in the validity of the EEL techniques and the evidence collecting by the evaluation methods. It was hoped that once this was established the staff would be able to take over the evaluation process themselves.

Evaluating Practice

The information gathered through observations, interviews, documentation and questionnaires provided a comprehensive and detailed picture of practice and provision in the day nursery. The curriculum offered a wide range of activities, some free and some structured. The children worked in large groups, in small groups or individually and all aspects of the children's development were encouraged. A set timetable of sessions existed and the day-by-day, week-to-week pattern of the Centre evolved around this timetable. As children arrived they assembled in the small carpeted room and the day always started with TV, a drink and a biscuit. After this the children moved on to free activities and, weather permitting, to outside play at 11.30 am. Individual Nursery Officers had the freedom to choose activities from day to day. Prior to the children's arrival in the morning, rooms were set out with a selected range of activities from the many available. All of these activities were open to all children and they worked at their own level depending on the activity.

Lunch was served between 12 and 1 pm, after which the children again were gathered in the small carpeted room for either story or TV. Then it was on to a soft play session in the large round room. By 2 pm all the staff had taken their lunch break and small group sessions then took place, but here particular children might be chosen for specific tasks. Again, the Nursery Officer leading

Children working at their own level in a variety of activities

the group decided on the activity, one preferring to have one child per activity each on separate tables, and another preferring to set up floor activities so that more children could be accommodated in a group. A Speech and Language Therapist visited the Centre twice a week for sessions with individuals or small groups of children.

An analysis of 130 recorded observations of activities over a period of two weeks showed the balance and range of curriculum areas experienced by the children. The most common activities were creative and aesthetic (45 observations), followed by language and literacy (38 observations), and physical: both fine and gross motor activity (26 observations). It was noted that, relatively, the children spent a lot of the time watching TV (12 observations). The least common activities were scientific (4 observations) and mathematical activities (7 observations). It should be pointed out that the children were offered other experiences than those observed, sometimes with a choice and at other times not. Also, it should be pointed out that these observations did not reflect the 'hidden curriculum' of children learning from the relationships built up with peers and adults, from the routines and patterns of the day, and from the values and attitudes of the Centre community. However, the 130 recorded observations did show that a range of activities were offered to the children, but that the children experienced some areas of the curriculum far more than others.

Key Workers at the Centre monitored the progress of 'their' children and the onus was on them to fill the gaps in the range of activities offered. 'Happenings' and individual children were discussed by the staff in the Centre at the end of each working day, and reviewed weekly by staff and parents of those families having Outreach. Team meetings and reviews, where parents, Key Workers and management met to discuss the progress of the child from the parents' and the Centre's point of view, occurred at longer intervals.

In the EEL Evaluation process, one measure of the quality of children's learning is through their observed level of Involvement in an activity. If children are fully absorbed, show persistence, purpose, enthusiasm and concentration, then it is likely that learning is taking place. Observing the children at the Centre engaged in a range of activities over a number of days using the Child Involvement Scale revealed their average levels of Involvement.

Figure 5.1 shows that a significant proportion of the children were observed to be operating at level 1 or 2 on the scale. Characteristically, this reveals the child displaying a lack of concentration, staring into space and easily distracted. The largest single proportion of children were observed at level 3, where a child

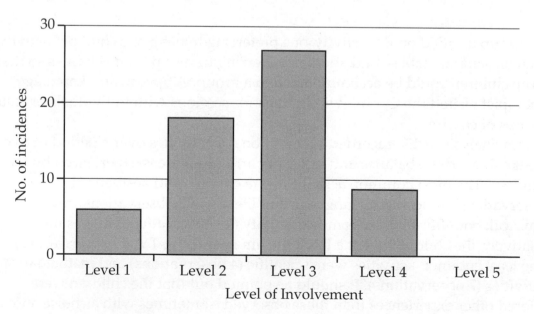

Figure 5.1   Involvements Levels of 3+ and 4+ year olds

is busy at an activity, but with routine actions and no real energy. The average of the observations, or the mean score for the Involvement levels of children in the Centre was 2.62. It is interesting to note that no incidence of level 5 Involvement was recorded.

The role of the adult is vital in determining the quality of the children's experiences. One member of staff saw her role as showing the children 'how to do and use different activities' and another as 'providing them (the children) with learning materials'. The Adult Engagement Scale classifies the adults' actions according to three kinds of input: Sensitivity, Stimulation and Autonomy. The staff were observed and their actions in each of the three categories were rated on a 5-point scale. This Scale was used to observe staff as they interacted with the children over a number of days and the scores of all the staff were amalgamated to produce an overall picture of the quality of the staff teams' interaction with the children.

The adult observations showed that the staff were generally sensitive to the children's emotional wellbeing and responsive to their needs. There was evidence of positive empathy where a child's feelings were supported and acknowledged, but also other instances where the child's feelings could have been responded to more sensitively or more appropriately. The staff gave plenty of praise, but this tended to be one-word responses such as the 'good', 'lovely' or 'nice' of busy people. There was little discussion or talk about the work, for example what made it good, or what was liked about it. The staff also gave the children much input to stimulate them, but often the input was of the 'closed' kind leading to routine responses by the children, and did not encourage the children to think, or act creatively or originally. Children were given very few opportunities for experimentation and independent action. The activities were often tightly structured with the adult intervening to direct the action in an approved way. The adults tended to take an authoritarian stance and solved problems themselves, rather than giving the child the chance for further negotiation to resolve conflict. There was little evidence of rules being explained to children, and often the child was corrected rather than his behaviour. Overall, the ability of the staff to give the children Autonomy was low.

ACTION PLANNING

Many valuable points and ideas were raised during the discussion which followed the presentation of the Evaluation Report to the staff. One member of staff was very surprised by the amount of time children spent watching TV. The children's interview comments were noted, and morale was boosted by the parents' positive interview responses. The most important point taken up by the staff was an increased awareness of the need for praise. In addition they saw that the children were not being given reasons for actions taken. This made the Deputy Manager realise that the staff had not been trained in the Behaviour Management course she ran for parents. At the end of the discussion important issues for further discussion were set down by the Manager as follows.

1   Look at our styles of intervention. Are we being too directive? Is it that there is not enough choice or do these children need more channelling because of their needs?
2   Look at the way we plan activities. Try more of a team approach and ensure that children do get a full range of activities.
3   Look at the consistency of our team approach to children's behaviour and work on a behaviour policy involving parents' views as well.
4   Note that we are developing as a Family Centre. We acknowledge that parents are the prime educators of their young children. We should be developing resource packs to increase parents' interaction with their children.

The Support Worker followed up these discussions by talking with the staff about ways of working with parents, and how they could further their expertise and training. Examples of materials useful for Outreach resource packs were borrowed for staff to look at. The Action Plan was written following two further meetings in which evidence presented in the Evaluation Report was discussed thoroughly, critiqued and reflected upon by all members of the staff. Finally it was agreed that a number of issues had emerged as deserving further development. These included the need to consider:

- ways of developing as a Family Centre, recognising that parents are the prime educators of their young children. Developing resource packs to help parents interact with their children;

- whole-team approaches to children's behaviour and to reviewing behaviour policy;

- the planning of activities;

- styles of intervention and interaction within the Centre.

The main aim was to plan training days covering these aspects of development, with the intention of establishing a whole-team approach within the Centre.

Training days, for team building and staff development, were held quite regularly at the Centre, and all staff including the cook, kitchen assistant and social worker participated. Four training days were available and the planned timescale for action was four months.

Improving Practice

All such training days started with an 'icebreaker' game, lighthearted but following the theme of the day. This aimed to relax everyone, and also helped them to focus their thinking. This was followed by a series of activities with everyone involved and contributing, in role-play, discussions, small group and whole group, brainstorming ideas, and giving feedback to the whole group.

Prior to the Action Plan one training day on 'Staff Confidence Building' and 'Working with Parents' had already been agreed, and during the last session of the second day the idea of Resource Packs for working at home with parents and children was introduced. The Resource Packs consisted of packages of ideas and activities, including all the necessary resources on a particular theme, or aspect of learning. They would be made available for use in the home on Outreach visits, so giving confidence to the Key Worker, and eliminating the last minute thinking of what to do and what equipment/activity to take on such a visit. The ideas were brainstormed and discussed by the group and a list of possible pack themes was drawn up. Then, in pairs, the group thought about the resources which could be needed and included in particular packs. This was felt to be a very worthwhile day which led very successfully into the following training day which was to be spent in making up the Resource Packs.

The day followed a similar pattern. Ideas were brainstormed and, in pairs, taking account of specialist knowledge and particular interests, packs were assembled. Each pair quickly became involved in discussion, collecting and sorting necessary resources for their packs. Lists were drawn up of resources needed, and expendable activity sheets were made for photocopying. At the end of the day the group shared their thoughts and ideas, showed their packs, and explained the reasons for inclusion of particular materials, and how they could be used. A real sense of achievement prevailed at the end of this day. The group had worked as a team and all had contributed in putting together some very useful resources, which would benefit everyone at the Centre.

The second training day was to focus on Behavioural Management. It was important that the staff should understand and experience the Behavioural Management course organised for parents. If the training was to follow the same pattern as that for parents', it would take one hour a week for nine weeks.

Sorting out how this could be organised was quite a problem. Eventually permission was granted by the Line Manager for one hour to be made available each Monday. Children would go home at 3 pm and not 4 pm as usual, and this hour was to be used by staff for training. This training proved to be very successful, so much so that the hour became a permanent feature each week for staff training. One Nursery Officer's hopes for the course were fulfilled. She felt the course encouraged the staff to work as a team, to support each other, and praise each other as they dealt with children and behaviours consistently. She also felt that the team could now more confidently act as role models, so helping parents put the content of the course into practice.

The third training day on Planning produced a great deal of useful discussion on routines and the daily or weekly pattern of activities and organisation of the Centre. In four groups the staff discussed areas where it was felt changes were needed. The groups came together and many ideas and suggestions were put forward. It was interesting that each group had concluded that they were in favour of more sessional care. Sessional care is where parents attend the Centre with their child and work in a one-to-one situation with the Key Worker. This was seen to be a very important issue, and if adopted by the Centre would mean changing its whole organisation. It could only be achieved very gradually, and maybe only then as part of the child's weekly programme of attendance. This topic dominated the discussion, and at the end of the day nothing definite had been decided, except that, where possible, there should be more sessional care as part of the Centre provision. It was felt that a great deal more time, thought and discussion would be necessary before anything could be finalised about such a major change.

The last training day was spent in compiling a Behaviour Policy for the Centre. Again the staff felt that this had been an excellent day, where they had worked as a team to develop this policy, discussing and agreeing strategies for consistent management of children throughout the day and for particular behaviours.

The effects of the EEL Project and the consequent Behaviour Management course led to the staff using positive praise much more when dealing with the children and each other. The response to this initiative was pleasing to see and hear. The atmosphere of the Centre was altogether calmer. The staff managed the children consistently and there was more positive interaction generally. These differences are reflected and recorded in the second round of child observations. Figure 5.2 shows the 3 and 4 year old children showed higher levels of involvement in their tasks and that they were not so easily distracted. The average level had risen from 2.62 to 3.25 with the majority of children operating on levels 3 and 4.

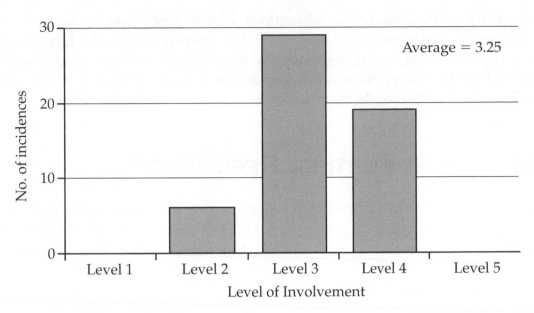

Figure 5.2   Involvement Levels of 3+ and 4+ year olds

The Adult Engagement observations also revealed a more positive style amongst the staff in their interactions with the children. They were dealing with the children more consistently and responding to their needs with a more 'open' style of Stimulation which encouraged the children to respond with more initiative and creativity.

REFLECTION ON ACTION

The staff at this setting were extremely hardworking young people who showed real affection for the children in their care. They were working long hours, for little pay, with children and families, all of whom had many problems. These young people took on great responsibilities, visiting the homes of children and being prepared to listen. Sometimes they were the only people around who would listen to all the worries of harassed parents. They did all this with great cheerfulness and dedication.

Participating in this Project required of the whole staff a level of professionalism and commitment which they gave willingly and with enthusiasm. They achieved a transformation of their practice within a relatively short timescale and had clear evidence that the actions they had taken improved the quality of experience they were able to offer their children, many of whom were at risk in the system. They all expressed feelings of personal and professional satisfaction and reward from their participation in the EEL Project. The Support Worker anticipates that these staff will go on to implement further developments of their practice and continue their pursuit of quality in the care and education of the children at the Centre.

ISSUES FOR FURTHER REFLECTION

This Case Study described how a team of nursery nurses in a social service day nursery worked together with an external Support Worker from the EEL Project to develop their provision. The resulting action focused on:

- developing their work with parents
- developing their behaviour management.

The processes they went through in achieving this improvement in their practice raise a number of important questions for discussion by those who work both within this type of setting and beyond.

1   How far is it desirable for children designated as needing special support to be catered for all together in specialist provision?

2   The importance of working in partnership with parents and families was acknowledged in this Centre. In what ways did the Centre facilitate this? Are there other strategies they might have used? Can formal Parent/Centre agreements help?

3   How can the limitations of multi-use centres be overcome?

4   The need to work at building a relationship between the 'insider' staff and the 'outsider' EEL Support Worker was evident in this case study. What are the difficulties with such a relationship and how might these be overcome? Do you feel an 'outsider' perspective is necessary?

5   How might the EEL Support Worker have acted to encourage the staff team to take on some of the observations and information gathering techniques themselves? What might the reasons be for their reluctance in taking this on?

6   How far did you agree with the focus for the chosen Action Plan? Were there other priorities they might have chosen?

7   What explanations might there be for the link between the level of Involvement of the children and the ways the adults were interacting with

them? Why did the level of children's Involvement go up in this Case Study? How far do you feel it was a result of the development of the staff?

8   Could the training days have been organised to make them more effective and developmental?

6 Case Study Six – A Nursery Class Within A Primary School

Janet Dye

Context

The nursery class which is the focus of this study formed part of a large primary school situated in an inner-city area of a large metropolitan authority. The children who attended this nursery class came from the immediate neighbourhood and many lived in high rise flats. There were fewer nursery places than were required in the area. The local population was predominantly made up of Bengali-speaking people from Bangladesh, and these children formed 85 per cent of the nursery intake. The nursery also had children from Somali, Arab, Philippino, Chinese, Sudanese and local British backgrounds on roll. Eighty-five to ninety per cent of the children entered the nursery as non-English speakers whose mothers also understood little or no English. Fathers who worked may have understood more English, but for many parents it was still at a basic level. However, most children acquired a working knowledge of English during their time in the nursery. Children usually attended the nursery from 3 to 5 years of age. Almost all of the forty children attended full-time, from 9.15 am to 3.15 pm during school terms. The children joined the main school just before their fifth birthday.

The physical environment

The primary school was surrounded by buildings, including shops, offices, blocks of flats and small hotels. There were large, walled asphalt play areas with appropriate markings and children's murals on inside walls. The school had a security entry system. The building was constructed in 1902 on three floors linked by tiled concrete stairways. Each floor had a hall with classrooms and cloakrooms leading from it. The nursery class comprised two connecting classrooms on the ground floor, with a self-contained toilet and cloakroom area nearby. It accommodated up to forty children full-time. A small part of the playground was fenced off for nursery use. An experienced headteacher had recently taken up the headship of the school.

The nursery had a wide range of equipment for children's indoor and outdoor use. The rooms were spacious, with high ceilings and windows, but were rather dark and in need of full cleaning, some redecoration and repair. Storage was limited and some materials also needed cleaning, repair and renewal. Outside, the playground had a fixed climbing frame, playhouse and storage for wheeled toys. The surface in this area was dusty and gritty and needed regular sweeping. There was one tree in the play area and open fencing revealed a small, overgrown wild garden which was part of the school property. The children could see the green plants, insects and the few birds which sometimes inhabited this area.

Staffing

The nursery was staffed by two qualified and experienced nursery teachers, one of whom was the nursery co-ordinator. There were also two qualified nursery nurses and one part-time bilingual support worker. During the period of the EEL Project, there was a Bengali speaking student working in the nursery for four days each week. One of the nursery nurses was absent for several weeks due to illness and a supply teacher was not always available. The nursery clerical and administrative work was carried out in the school office and lunches were provided by the local authority school meals service. Teachers and nursery nurses were responsible for children at lunchtime and for serving the meal. A general assistant from the school worked in the nursery for one hour at lunchtimes to enable staff to have a short break.

Organisation in the nursery

The nursery class shared the aims and objectives written for the whole school, and staff had begun writing a specific statement of aims for the nursery to be incorporated into a booklet for parents. The nursery offered children a full curriculum, covering human and social learning, language and literacy, mathematics, science and technology, physical education and creative and aesthetic education. The staff had regular meetings to discuss curriculum development and produce topic planning webs to cover the main National Curriculum subject framework. Topics usually lasted from two to six weeks. Planning included aims, organisation starting points, special resources and assessment. Children's visits were included whenever possible. On a weekly and daily basis, the general activities were planned, the organisation of key experiences agreed and staff responsibilities were decided. Whilst particular adults were working with a small group or a particular child on key

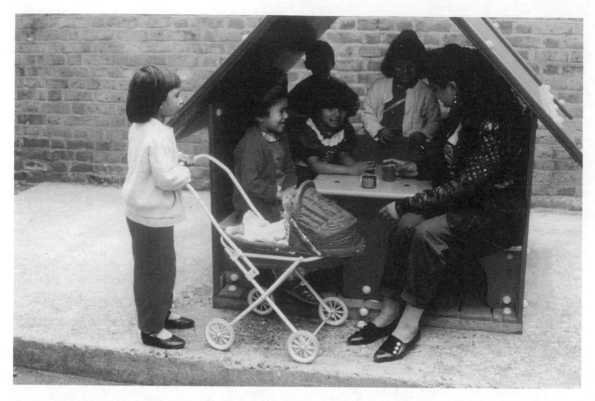

Adults sometimes joined in children's play to extend and develop it

experiences, the other adults often took a supervisory role. Nursery teachers also attended school staff meetings.

The children's day began at 9.15 am when they excitedly entered the nursery with parents and carers. They could choose from a full range of indoor activities until 10 am when outdoor activities were included. Some children worked in turn with staff on key experiences. Milk was available at any time. At 10.45 clearing up began, ready for story in two groups at 11.05. At 11.20 children were supervised in the washroom ready for lunch at 11.30 am. Between 11.30 and 12.30, lunch was served in the nursery and all staff ate here. From 12.30 to 1.30 activities were organised by the school general assistant and some staff, while others had a half-hour lunch break. At 1.30 pm the afternoon session began with a full range of indoor and outdoor activities. Again some children worked on key experiences. At 2.30 pm adults and children cleared up before fruit or biscuits were served for tea. Stories were then told to two or three groups before parents came to collect children at 3.15 pm.

Strategies For Working Together

After initial meetings with the headteacher and nursery co-ordinator to discuss the nursery participation, the EEL Support Worker met the whole nursery staff to explain the Project and enlist their support and cooperation. This meeting covered the Project timetable and discussion of the support required. During the Project, all the adults in the nursery cooperated in giving information, gathering data and taking part in informal discussions and meetings. The headteacher fully supported the work and later encouraged participants to share the findings with all the primary school staff.

A realistic timetable was agreed by the EEL Support Worker and participants to ensure that the Project kept on schedule and maintained participants' initial enthusiasm and momentum. It was agreed that collection of the factual information about the setting, the interviews with nursery staff, and interviews with parents and children, should be completed within six weeks. The nursery co-ordinator arranged for all the nursery staff to help gather the information including lists of equipment, layout plans, curriculum documents, the school development plan, details of financial expenditure and other information needed to set the class in context. Each person had particular tasks to complete which were related to his or her own experience and area of responsibility.

Suitable times were arranged for the EEL Support Worker to interview teachers and nursery nurses, as well as the headteacher. Interviews generally lasted twenty minutes or more and were carried out before and after school sessions and during lunchtime. On one occasion when the school was locked at the end of the day, we moved to a nearby café to complete our discussions. Parents were interviewed by the EEL Support Worker and the interviews were arranged to coincide with children's arrival or collection from school. Sometimes several parents were interviewed together to increase their confidence. Children were informally interviewed in twos or threes by the EEL Support Worker, a member of staff or the bilingual support worker. This was arranged at convenient times during the day so that children did not miss favourite or popular activities. Discussions were carried out in a quiet library area of the nursery so there were few distractions.

The organisation of the observation of children and adults in the setting was discussed. Initially, the EEL Support Worker carried out Child Tracking and Child Involvement observations. After seeing the work involved, both nursery nurses and teachers helped to observe particular children in a range of situations and made some records. The bilingual support worker and bilingual student also joined in this work. Sometimes this took the form of undertaking observation, sometimes it involved ensuring a colleague or the EEL Support Worker was free to observe and was not unduly contacted by children or others.

The observation of adults was carried out by the EEL Support Worker, as the nursery co-ordinator judged that it would be inappropriate for all the staff to observe each other in a structured manner. The staff were happy for the EEL Support Worker and nursery co-ordinator to carry out the observations. The staff were also reassured to know that no particular person would be identified in the study and that Adult Engagement observations would be compiled for the setting as a whole. Adults were informed that we would be observing adults and children during a session but not the exact time of the observation. This helped to diffuse their initial anxiety about being observed. The nursery co-ordinator made sure everyone felt at ease with this and all adults were happy to participate. In fact, most observations of adults were carried out by the EEL Support Worker.

In a short space of time, by working together, the EEL Support Worker and all the adults in the nursery managed to compile a great deal of information about the setting. Both the observations of children and those of adults were carried out within the agreed timescale of six weeks. The school/nursery factual information, and the longer term planning and record keeping information were analysed by the EEL Support Worker, who also made careful observations of the day-to-day organisation and management of the work of the nursery. The regular meetings arranged with all the staff ensured all views could be considered, particularly those of part-time staff and nursery nurses, and they gave appropriate opportunities for feedback and dialogue. It was important to arrange meetings well in advance, to have a known agenda and to start and finish on time. However, informal discussions, comments and questions proved as important as the formally organised meetings. The EEL Support Worker made time to listen to staff concerns, whether they were linked to the Project or not, to note their achievements, to observe and talk with children and parents and to join in the life of the nursery as much as possible.

EVALUATING PRACTICE

Interviews with staff showed that they had shared aims and objectives and language learning was a high priority in the provision of a broad and balanced curriculum. The staff work hard to provide the full range of the curriculum and to help all children to understand English. Interviews with parents showed they were happy with the education and care provided and pleased with their children's development and attitudes to learning. They said they would like

Children cooperated well together

more information about the curriculum. When interviewed, children were able to talk at length about a range of activities which they enjoyed, including building, drawing, singing, work with sand, water, talking with teachers and outdoor play. Their dislikes were comparatively few, relating to quarrels, lunchtime arrangements and lotto games with structured language practice. It was clear that the nursery class provided a secure and caring place for young children's learning.

The observation of children's Involvement levels showed that children achieved an average of 2.95 on a scale of 1 to 5, and were most involved when they had some input from sources outside themselves, for example stories, teacher talk, looking at books, joining in music, sensory inputs from sand, water, motor play. They also showed high levels of Involvement when engaged in imaginary play, in freely chosen creative work such as drawing and colouring, junk modelling, problem solving, exploratory play and in talking with and helping an adult. The observations showed that children were least involved when tired, upset or they wished to rest. They then wandered aimlessly or drifted to a solitary activity. There was low Involvement when an activity became crowded or when the materials available offered little new challenge. Clearly, there was need for more quiet times and rest. The observations revealed the need for a wider range of books, also increased provision for particular aspects of mathematics and science, and that more time was needed for adults to join in children's self-chosen activities and develop the work. Children were only able to be deeply involved for about 2.5 hours a day when all activities were available and fully staffed, together with 0.75 hours of grouptime. The lunch period effectively took two hours from 11.30 to 1.30. The observations showed it was difficult for tired children to rest in a busy nursery environment and the strain of learning to use another language for a long period led to frustration and tiredness in the afternoons.

The Adult Engagement observations showed marked variations in the Stimulation aspect of the adults' behaviour. Most adult talk centred round the correction of language, introducing activities and ensuring successful participation. This is almost inevitable when children are learning a second language. The observations showed that sometimes adults were warm and showed empathy with children and responded easily, whilst at other times they were less sensitive to children's needs and used less positive and supportive language. The picture was also varied when Autonomy was observed. Sometimes staff found it easy to let the children lead, share experiences and to draw out children's ideas and thoughts. At other times they found it more difficult and sometimes saw their role as telling, correcting or organising, and this could occasionally lead to negative statements or loud instructions which appeared worrying or confusing to some children. There appeared some inconsistency in the application of rules and routines relating to the codes of conduct agreed by the seven adults with whom the children had daily contact. The observations also showed that adults in the nursery had a demanding task, as they were helping almost all children to learn English as well as to utilise the learning opportunities offered in the nursery.

General observation of a range of particular activities offered in the nursery also confirmed that some children needed very basic help in handling tools, scissors, glue and other materials. They also needed very sensitive help to encourage them to persist in mastering fine motor skills. Children who were involved in a self-chosen activity, or imaginative play for a sustained period, sometimes received insufficient adult support to help them develop and extend the work. However, when activities were set up by adults as part of key experiences or topics, they were very thoroughly extended, but children were often less enthusiastic and involved than when their own ideas and interest were used as starting points for learning.

ACTION PLANNING

The background information, interviews and observations were documented into an Evaluation Report by the EEL Support Worker. All participants agreed this was an accurate picture of the nursery class. Several meetings were held so that the nursery staff, with the support of the headteacher, could formulate an Action Plan to address some of the highlighted matters. Shortly after the Evaluation Report was produced, the headteacher and staff made some key decisions concerning the admissions policy and future structure of the school day. It was decided to introduce part-time admission, so most children would attend for 2.5 hours daily, giving more children an opportunity to attend the nursery class. Some older children would continue to attend full-time and the part-time policy would be introduced for most new admissions. The changes meant that the morning session lasted from 9.00 to 11.30 am, the afternoon session from 12.45 to 3.15 pm and lunch was taken at 11.45 am in the parents' room in the main school. This enabled staff to prepare afternoon activities and organise their breaks so that all were present to start the afternoon session at 12.45 pm.

The headteacher, with the support of the staff, arranged for more storage shelving to be provided and more rugs for storytime and floor activities. Internal redecoration, resurfacing of the outside play area and refurbishment of the wild garden were included in future whole-school expenditure plans. Some minor repairs to windows and walls were carried out. The nursery staff then discussed other matters raised in the Evaluation Report and together with the EEL Support Worker made an Action Plan with targets for one to two months, for four to six months and for a year or more. All staff participated in the discussion, which took several meetings and all agreed to support the work. The Action Plan thus had three sections.

Short-term goals

1   the provision of more picture reference books about life in Britain and overseas, and more dual language early reading books;
2   reorganisation of role-play materials and development of particular role-play situations;
3   ensuring that drawing, cutting and sticking and fine motor control activities are always available and all children are encouraged to participate;
4   outside area play markings begun to encourage more thoughtful use of equipment and ensure equal opportunity for access to all resources.

Medium-term goals

1   the provision of more mathematical experience;
2   organisation of staff training and visits;
3   developing better consistency of expectation;
4   achieving improved observation and record keeping.

Long-term goals

1   production of a dual language booklet for parents, with photographs showing the work of the nursery;
2   the production of a curriculum document for the nursery;
3   organising greater contact with parents, including more regular open sessions to discuss their children's development, asking them to share a skill and join children for local visits;
4   arranging more contact between the staff of the nursery and that of the school.

It was recognised that these were ambitious goals but the nursery team wished to address all the important issues raised in the Evaluation Report as part of their ongoing commitment to the development of the work of the nursery.

Following the agreement of the Action Plan the whole team attended a day conference and arranged to visit other nurseries in pairs. They also held discussions concerning adult style and consistency and agreed to try to fully implement the agreed code of conduct for adults and children. The whole team agreed it was everyone's responsibility to observe and monitor children's achievements. The nursery co-ordinator agreed to produce a draft new record folder for the children to be discussed by staff.

IMPROVING PRACTICE

The short-term goals of the Action Plan were managed within the time allocated. Books were borrowed from the main school library and others were ordered for the nursery. The headteacher made funds available to purchase additional materials and staff reorganised books and materials in the summer holiday. The role-play materials were rearranged so that materials to extend play were readily available and clothes and other props could successfully be used and tidied. During the new term, staff began implementing the Action Plan, making sure that drawing, sticking and fine motor control activities were always readily available

Indoor and outdoor activities were further developed

and all children were encouraged to develop and practice their skills. It was felt to be particularly important to encourage some boys to develop these skills, whilst also encouraging girls to develop skills using wheeled toys outside. It was not always easy for all staff to keep to the agreed approach as some children needed considerable support to help them try different activities. Sometimes the work was interrupted by staff absence and available supply staff having less knowledge of the children and nursery staff expectations.

Staff training and visits were organised as part of the medium-term goal as the headteacher arranged some supply staff. All staff attended a day conference and series of evening meetings on early education. Teachers, nursery nurses and the language support worker made half-day visits in pairs to two other nurseries. Their observations focused on organisation and management, planning the curriculum, work with parents and resources. They reported back to colleagues at staff meetings. The nursery co-ordinator, supported by the headteacher, took a lead to ensure that all staff actively carried out the code of conduct relating to consistency in establishing acceptable behaviour by children and maintaining a calm approach by all adults. They gave necessary support to children and adults and plentiful praise for achievement. Progress was sometimes uncertain, often slow but nevertheless change gradually happened and the children and adults could see the benefit of a quieter, calmer atmosphere, particularly at clearing-up times. Children became more confident as they understood how many were allowed at activities, how to tidy-up effectively and cooperate with adults.

Progress also occurred on the long-term goals. Photographs were taken ready for the booklet for parents and a draft text was compiled. Production of the booklet was delayed by shortage of school clerical staff time. The nursery co-ordinator had also produced a draft record of achievement for discussion. Nursery staff attended a school staff meeting, and the headteacher also planned some meetings for the nursery staff to meet with Year 1 and Year 2 teachers to discuss the curriculum and its co-ordination from the nursery to the main school. Parents were invited to join the staff and children on local visits and to share a skill. They were also asked to attend informal open sessions to discuss their child's development. This increased contact was much appreciated and the visit to a local zoo with many parents accompanying children was memorable as it was also a first visit for many of the parents.

The staff were very pleased with the outcome of their activities. In the new term, they really felt the benefit of the change to part-time provision for most children. The new lunchtime arrangements gave them opportunity to prepare for afternoon work. The new rugs, storage and improvements to books, equipment and decor were greatly appreciated. The children too were calmer, more deeply involved and orderly as staff were more consistent in their expectations. The nursery nurses and support staff said they felt more fully involved in the planning and decision-making in the nursery and they appreciated the greater contact with school staff and visits to other nurseries. They had made progress in all the areas they had identified and were pleased with the outcomes of their hard work.

REFLECTION ON ACTION

The children's parents were pleased with the developments in the nursery. They were delighted that they had more contact with the staff, were able to join their children on local visits and were sometimes asked to share a skill with a group of children. Although some parents wished their children to attend full-time, they understood the reason for the change. Parents enjoyed looking at and discussing photographs of their children working at a range of curriculum activities and more began to understand the reason for the activities.

The children had a wider range of curriculum activities regularly available, particularly those for mathematics, science and focused role-play. Their level of Involvement increased significantly over the period of the EEL Project. The average score increased by more than one level to 4, which showed that children had much deeper levels of intense concentration, enthusiasm and persistence at an activity than at the start of the Project. They became more purposeful and calm in their approach to all activities as the rules and routines of the nursery were consistently applied. Children were able to talk about a greater range of activities which they enjoyed.

The staff cooperated well together to promote the changes they had agreed upon. They gave freely of their own time during the summer holiday, and after school during term time, to reorganise the materials, discuss and plan the curriculum, plan new developments and meet with colleagues and parents. They appreciated the support given to their work by the headteacher, particularly in allocating funds for materials, books and equipment and organising supply cover to enable them to visit other settings. The organisational changes at lunchtime and the move to part-time education were also seen as fully supportive of their core work and undoubtedly kept their morale high, as their work was more publicly valued within the school community. Without the financial support provided by the school, many of the changes and developments in practice would have been very difficult.

The quality of children's learning had improved in many ways over the period of the Project. The children had increased time and opportunity in each session to develop their own ideas and learning. Observation showed that the curriculum had increased in breadth and the organisation of the adults provided more time for them to talk with children individually and in small groups and to extend the work. Equal opportunities were more consistently given to boys and girls in indoor and outdoor activities. The children's level of Involvement increased and the Adult Engagement observations showed adults being more sensitive and stimulating in their responses to children: listening, smiling and encouraging them to talk. This increase in positive approaches shows the change in the overall pattern of adult interaction. The children's response to these changes in adult style was also clear and was reflected in their increasing talk and the calm, purposeful atmosphere in the nursery.

All the work that the staff undertook in planning the layout of the nursery, increasing the provision of books, materials and the range of regular supported activities and in promoting a calm and consistent environment contributed to the children's deeper Involvement in their activities. A great deal was achieved in just 10 months and, most importantly, the work continued after this initial phase of development. The EEL Project proved a most valuable means of helping adults become increasingly reflective practitioners in order to extend the learning of the children in their care. Undoubtedly, the children, the school and the wider community benefited from the achievements of this group of nursery practitioners.

ISSUES FOR FURTHER REFLECTION

This Case Study describes how a team of practitioners in a nursery class of a large primary school collaborated with an EEL Support Worker to evaluate critically the quality of their provision. Their evaluation led them to focus their development on:

- developing materials and resources;
- improving the outside play area;
- providing a broader range of learning experiences;
- staff development;
- enhancing parental partnership.

The processes they went through in achieving this improvement in their practice raise a number of important questions for discussion by those who work both within this type of setting and beyond.

1   This nursery class changed from full- to part-time. Was this a change for the better and why?
2   The EEL Support Worker collaborated fully with the nursery team. How might she have developed this collaboration further?
3   Should adult observations be carried out by an insider or outsider? What are the issues involved here?
4   How might young children be helped to express their voice in an evaluation process? What strategies might be used?
5   The children's Involvement level went up dramatically in this setting. What contributed to this increase?
6   How useful are visits to other nurseries as a means of staff development?
7   The adults worked hard to create a calmer, more positive atmosphere in the nursery. What are the factors that affect this?
8   What are the basic essentials of equipment and resources in a nursery class?
9   What are the pressures of working in a nursery within a primary school? What are the benefits?

7 CASE STUDY SEVEN – A PRIVATE DAY NURSERY

Fiona Ramsden

CONTEXT

This private day nursery was opened in July 1990 by its current owner. It was situated in a bungalow in a quiet cul-de-sac in a city suburb. The premises had been refurbished to the present owner's specifications for a day nursery. The children could attend the nursery from the age of 2 years until 5 years. There was a maximum of 24 places per day – Monday to Friday from 8.15 am–5.30 pm. Apart from bank holidays the nursery was only closed for two weeks in the summer. The catchment area of the nursery covered the city and surrounding rural area. Forty-three per cent of parents were from a professional background, 39 per cent from skilled, 14 per cent from semi-skilled and 4 per cent unemployed. Of the 35 children who attended the nursery, eight were 2 years old, 15 were 3 years old and 12 were 4 years old. 6 per cent were from ethnic minority families and 23 per cent from one-parent families.

It was clear from the nursery's policy documents that the aim of the nursery, as stated in the brochure was to:

> . . . *provide high quality full day care and education for groups of children aged 2–5 years* through *a safe, secure, yet exciting environment for young children.*

Establishing the importance of play as a means of children learning was also a very clear aim of the nursery. Indeed the brochure stated, 'Play is vital for a child's normal development'.

The staff clearly also held this aim as one member stated at interview, the aim of the nursery was, 'to supply a happy atmosphere where children can learn through play'.

The nursery day

The day began at 8.15 am, with flexible provision for parents to extend this until 10.00 am. The children started with free play in one playroom, until they had all arrived, and then they divided into separate rooms for milk and biscuit time. The younger children all sat around a table with the staff and had a story and a chat. The children walked daily to the nearby shops, or to the local library, the play area or the river. If the weather was inclement they played inside the nursery with a variety of activities which may have included sand and water.

Meanwhile the older children had stories, constructive play and cooking in the kitchen, with a walk at about 11.00. Lunch was at approximately 12.00, and all children and staff sat down together for a home-cooked meal. Afterwards one playroom was organised for children who required a nap, until about 2.30 pm or when they woke up. There were quiet table activities and games for the non-sleepers in the other playroom.

All the children and staff then joined up for a group activity, such as physical exercises, playing musical instruments, or a short walk to feed the swans (the nursery supported the local swan sanctuary) at the nearby riverside. Tea was at 3.45 and then there was free play as the parents started to arrive from 4.00 until 5.30, when the nursery closed.

Physical environment and facilities

The staff and owner of the nursery felt it was very important that the physical environment served the children's needs. The bungalow had been purposefully adapted to accommodate a day nursery to the owner's recommendations: 'to give a safe, secure yet exciting environment for young children'. The staff felt that the nursery served the children's needs by providing, 'a homely environment', 'places to be quiet', 'the garden for more noise', 'time to be on their own', 'times to be organised and times when not', 'a comfy chair for a cuddle', 'a learning environment with sand, water and dressing-up clothes'.

The parents felt that 'separate rooms were useful with places for different items so children learn to put things away'. One parent felt that 'fresh air, space and exercise' were fundamental to a child's wellbeing, and that this was difficult for the nursery to provide particularly in winter and bad weather. The children were not specifically asked about the physical environment but instead they were asked to draw anything that they particularly enjoyed at the nursery. Their pictures showed that they all greatly enjoyed playing outside in the garden and that playing ball was a particular favourite.

The inside of the nursery consisted of two playrooms, Playroom 1 for the under-3s, and Playroom 2 for the 3–5 year olds (see Figures 7.1, 7.2 and 7.3). The environment was colourful, with children's own artwork displayed in murals on the walls. It was a clean, warm, comfortable and safe environment. The furniture was child-sized, in good repair and there were individual facilities for

Katy's playing ball

the children's belongings. Both rooms had a combination of a carpeted area and a washable floor. Playroom 1 had a settee for the younger children. Each playroom had toys and activities depending on the age and development of the children and these were laid out on child-sized tables and on the floor. Books were available in both rooms on low shelves. The foyer area and office were also utilised as temporary space for small groups of children to sit around a table with one member of staff in order to play games, draw and chat, in one-to-one combinations and small groups.

Toilets and sinks were child-sized, safe and allowed privacy. Meals and snacks were cooked on the premises and were nutritious. The children were provided with meals on tables, laid by themselves and an adult, with tablecloths and child-sized cutlery. All the staff sat down to eat meals and snacks with the children. The kitchen was kept secure with a bolted stable door, which allowed the children to be able to see the cook and yet provided safety too. The kitchen was used by small groups of children with an adult for cooking activities.

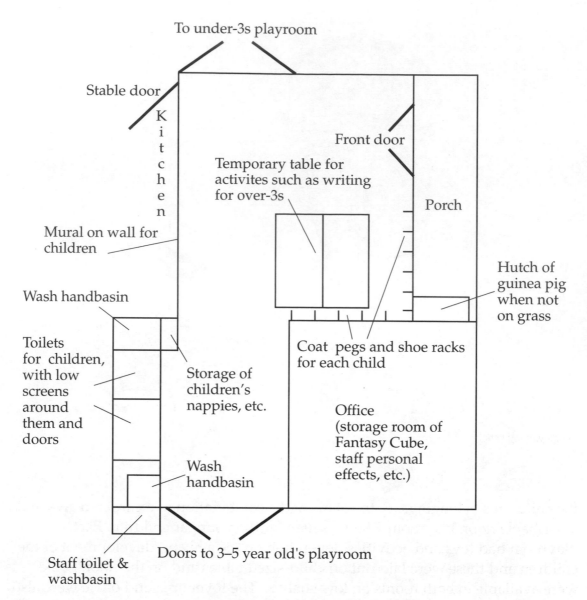

To under-3s playroom

Stable door

K
i
t
c
h
e
n

Front door

Temporary table for
activites such as writing
for over-3s

Porch

Mural on wall for
children

Hutch of
guinea pig
when not
on grass

Wash handbasin

Toilets
for children,
with low
screens
around
them and
doors

Storage of
children's
nappies, etc.

Coat pegs and shoe racks
for each child

Office
(storage room of
Fantasy Cube,
staff personal
effects, etc.)

Wash
handbasin

Staff toilet &
washbasin

Doors to 3–5 year old's playroom

Figure 7.1   Plan of nursery foyer leading to kitchen area, office, toilet block and porch

The outside area consisted of a mature garden with a grass surface and a secure fence surrounding it. There was a climbing frame, swings, a vegetable plot used by the children to grow their own vegetables and a guinea pig in a hutch. Facilities such as the sand or water trough, the home corner equipment and tables and chairs were taken out of the main nursery building in fine weather and placed in the garden.

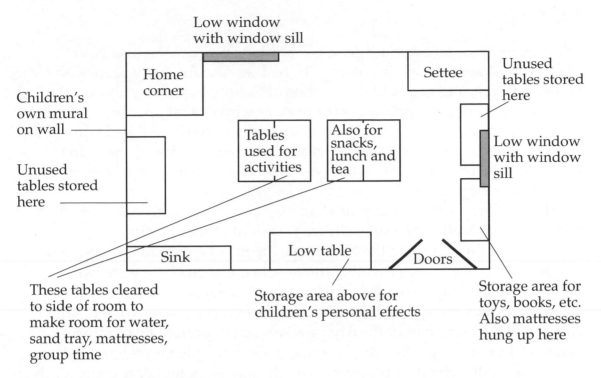

Figure 7.2   *Plan of playroom 1 – under-3s*

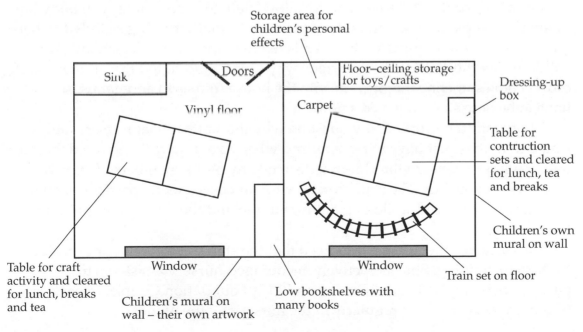

Figure 7.3   *Plan of playroom 2 – over-3s*

Staffing

The nursery was staffed with one active, working owner, who held NNEB, RSCN and Montessori qualifications. She had worked for many years with young children, and had held the position of County Under-5s Advisor. She had formulated the original policies of the nursery when it first opened. However, from that time minor issues had been discussed and communicated with all the staff, at meetings held at regular intervals. Since the owner was a working member of the nursery she was always available if staff or parents needed to discuss anything with her.

The manager of the nursery also had long experience with young children and held the NNEB qualification. There were four other nursery nurses/assistants: one held the NNEB, one the PLA Foundation Course and was first aid trained, and two other trainees. In addition, there were two members of staff who provided a home-cooked lunch and tea each day and ensured the nursery was cleaned. The cook/housekeeper also worked with the children in the latter part of the day, providing an important link for the children. The nursery was active in training YTS and college students and one student actually gained employment with the nursery after her training. Each member of staff was allocated to one particular room in order to provide continuity for the children.

From the interviews carried out as part of the EEL process, the staff saw their role as 'to be there for the children', 'to prepare a safe and stimulating environment for the children', and to 'allow them to grow not only in body but in mind'. The parents saw the role of the staff as 'motherly/big sisterly teachers' who 'can be more familiar with the children than the teacher in school'. The children saw the staff's role in various ways. One child noted that 'if they (staff) didn't come someone might come into the house (nursery) and get us, so they have to be here so no-one takes us away'.

Other children didn't really question why the staff were at nursery and stated that 'they just have to be here' and when asked 'why?' answered 'because they ought to'. None of the children disliked any of the members of staff, but many had favourites. The staff worked very much as a team, particularly with regard to the care and wellbeing of the children and the day-to-day running of the nursery.

The owner of the nursery was keen that the staff were given opportunities for further training. She had actively encouraged nursery assistants to participate in the NVQ qualification and PLA Foundation Course. In-service training was carried out regularly in the nursery by the owner.

Strategies For Working Together

Initially the nursery owner was approached by myself, as an EEL Support Worker, to ask if she would consider taking part in the project. She leapt at the chance of being involved and in particular wanted to participate in the EEL Quality Evaluation and Development process. After initial discussions with the owner it was felt to be very important that all the nursery staff should be involved in the process, as they worked as a team. Therefore the entire staff were present at all meetings and discussions regarding the Project. More importantly the ideas of the nursery staff were encouraged and each member was made to feel that her or his ideas were valued.

Although a large proportion of the data was collected by the EEL Support Worker, the participants, particularly the staff, were shown the data at every stage and we discussed what had been seen and recorded that session. This meant that the practitioners became gradually more and more interested in the Project because they recognised its implications for their practice. In fact, it was not only the staff who talked about the Project but obviously many of the children were intrigued. Even though it had been explained to them initially they still asked 'what are you doing that for?' at various times, to which the Support Worker felt an honest answer was warranted. On many occasions, the children would join in and carry out their own observations on 'one of your special sheets'.

During the Evaluation and Development process, the owner, staff, and manager of the nursery received training in the Child Involvement Scale and they were given the opportunity to carry out all aspects of the data collection. Some of the staff, after some initial anxiety caused essentially by uncertainty and fear of 'doing it wrong', carried out the observations and found them most rewarding. On one occasion a nursery assistant was sitting near to the Support Worker as she observed a child and afterwards they discussed the observation. She became very interested and decided that she would 'have a go'. After a short time, she returned, amazed at the amount she had learnt in a short but focused observation of one child, and she said, 'I can't believe how much I normally miss.' She felt intrigued and inspired to continue observing the children she felt she knew so well. This scenario provided clear evidence that it is more valuable to the practitioners if they themselves carry out at least some of the data collection. Gradually all the staff became very keen to participate in collecting the data and also wanted to share their thoughts on what they observed. This definitely helped in the establishment of a good collaborative working relationship. It was realised that already the Quality Evaluation and Development Process was starting to affect practice in the nursery.

There were a number of successes to celebrate:

- **Aims and objectives.** The staff and owner's aim, to provide a 'warm', 'caring', 'friendly' and 'homely atmosphere' for the children was achieved by the smell of home cooking which pervaded the nursery, the setting of the bungalow in a mature garden, the size of the rooms, the low windows for the children to look out, and the armchair. These features helped to provide a stable and secure context from which children can learn.

- **Curriculum.** The aim of the nursery curriculum was for children to learn through play, as expressed by the owner, 'the environment or "stage" is set up for children to learn, and the staff take on the role of stage manager'. The adult observations indicated that the setting did provide a very sensitive environment for the children, with a high incidence of adults being responsive, providing individual attention for the children and encouraging child-initiated talk.

- **Learning and teaching styles.** There was clear evidence that 'learning' can be linked favourably with the degree of Involvement that children exhibit. Laevers (1994(b)) has shown that a child is more likely to be learning if he shows signals of high involvement, i.e. concentration, persistence, creativity and precision. However the staff and parents, quite rightly, wanted the Evaluation Report to clearly state that a child cannot always be functioning at a high level 5: children need 'time out'. The Involvement levels for the nursery were collated and revealed that there was a high occurrence of levels 4 and 5 Involvement at the nursery. Indeed it constituted 56 per cent of the total number of incidences we observed. The average level of Involvement for the setting was 3.53. This was a high average.

- **Relationships and interaction.** The social development of the children was felt to be one of the prime aims of the nursery held by all participants in the setting. The Target Child observations supported this aim as it recorded interactions between target children and their peers, and target children and adults. The resultant data indicated that 56 per cent of interactions were between children and 44 per cent were with an adult. Eighty-four per cent of the interactions were positive in tone. The children's interviews and the Involvement observations showed that there was clearly a bonding between many of the children and the staff. Most children had a favourite member of staff. The children all knew each other well and had 'best' friends too. Importantly, one member of staff noted 'the staff care about each other and this provides a caring atmosphere for the children'.

- **Parental partnership.** The Evaluation Report indicated, through an analysis of the interviews with the parents, that the owner's aim to promote parental involvement was achieved and greatly appreciated by all concerned. As one parent indicated, 'I do feel I could go in anytime if I wanted'. The parents interviewed felt quality was ensured by this 'open door approach', and one parent noted 'the nursery is not afraid of visitors and parents coming in'. Another parent noted that there was no need to have records kept or meetings to discuss the children, as 'we can talk about things anytime'.

- **Community liaison.** The nursery made a positive effort to make the children aware of the local community. There were regular visits made to the nursery by a policewoman known as Tina to the children. The staff and children regularly walked to the local library, shops, the park and into the nearby city. The nursery took an active interest in the protected swan sanctuary on the nearby river and the children walked there to feed the birds.

ACTION PLANNING

As indicated earlier, as soon as the practitioners started on the Evaluation and Development Process they began to think about their practice. However it was at an Action Planning meeting held one evening with all the staff present that many issues and concerns were raised as a result of the Evaluation Report. It was felt to be important that the staff did not take on too much all at once and so a number of aspects were outlined which were felt by the staff to be worthy of development.

1   The staff were aware, after using the Child Involvement Scale themselves, that they needed to observe individual children, rather than the whole group as before. As one staff member stated, 'We need to observe more and be more focused.'
2   As a consequence of the interviews with parents it came to light that many parents would like more information about the staff and their roles, particularly as the nursery had a regular flow of visitors. As one parent wrote after reading the Evaluation Report,

You don't play up your staff enough. I did know Ms G. was doing a NVQ but I couldn't place the others, and information on when staff leave and who replaces them would be good.

3   As a consequence of a combination of the results of the Child Tracking data (outlined below), the adult observations and the interviews, the staff decided that they wanted to provide the children with more Autonomy. The individual Child Tracking data had indicated that within the Zone of Initiative or level of free choice, the children had only a limited amount of choice in their own selection of an activity. The children were guided by the activities that were placed out for them by the staff. One child who was interviewed obviously was not unduly concerned by the lack of Autonomy provided as he stated,

Yes, they do tell you what you can and can't do . . . you can't do everything so they put things out that you really like best – like the water!

Child Tracking research data: zone of initiative

Level	Description of level	No. of incidence
Level 1	No choice for the child	15
Level 2	Limited choices	35
Level 3	Some activities are excluded	–
Level 4	Child has freedom of choice	–

The Adult Engagement observations were also collated to indicate the overall style of the team of adults within the setting. The staff were responsive to the children but generally there were fewer observed incidents of giving Autonomy. It was clear that the children see the rules set by the adults to be obeyed, as one child noted, 'We do have rules 'cos there's things you must and must not do'.

4   As a result of the interviews and observations of children the staff decided that they wanted to ensure all areas of the curriculum were well provided for. The interviews had shown that all of the staff felt that the nursery covered most areas of the curriculum but as one member stated, 'we cover most areas but not so much physical'. The parents interviewed were unsure what the curriculum should entail at this age but they were very certain that it should, as one parent stated,

. . . focus on something in which they (the children) are interested and build around it. Unlike at school where they must *cover certain ground.*

There was also great importance placed by the parents on the 'socialisation' of the child above a set subject-based curriculum. However, it is difficult in any early years setting to define exactly what children are learning. They can often experience a wide range and variety of activities at any one time. For example, a water trough can provide science, mathematics, role-play, creative, social and language experiences for a young child. Observations revealed that in the nursery the most frequent curriculum areas covered were human/social and language/literacy. The nursery did not possess a computer so obviously this was an area that was not covered.

5   The staff and manager decided that they would experiment with the layout of the nursery in order to provide the children with more Autonomy and freedom of movement. This was a real change as they had worked with the same layout since the nursery had opened. As the manager originally stated,

> *The layout indicated on the plan is the layout which works well with 24 children in the building. We try not to change things too often as children feel more secure in a stable environment.*

Any small changes in layout that did take place were temporary movements, for example tables and chairs stacked to one side of the playrooms to make way for the sand/water trough and for mattresses at nap time.

Improving Practice

The practitioners decided on the areas that they wanted to improve and wrote an Action Plan which set out their aims and objectives and strategies. The Plan explained who would be responsible for each small part of the action and supplied a timescale. Once the Action Plan had been agreed by all the staff in the nursery then each member was provided with his or her own copy. This enabled all the participants to feel they had a part to play in the action.

The following is a brief outline of the action that took place in the nursery.

1 Observations

All of the staff, having received Involvement training, began to carry out observations of individual children on a regular basis. Through these observations staff were more able to ensure that the developmental needs of individual children as well as the group were met. As a result of the above observations the staff became aware that the early morning session needed replanning. The children arrived at different times in the morning which caused a problem with staffing and was having a negative effect upon the children. A vignette was written by a member of staff to summarise the powerful effect that an experiment on the early morning programme had upon the whole nursery.

Catherine's Vignette

Context

At the nursery in the morning from the time of opening at 8.15 am until 9.30 am, the children arrive at any time to suit their parents' needs. Although obviously very helpful to the parents, this causes the nursery difficulty in terms of staffing. For this reason the children and staff were all in one room until everyone had arrived when they dispersed to their own rooms. I felt from my observations that this was not a very peaceful welcome for the children and that all being in one room was too crowded and noisy.

My hopes

I wanted to make the children's arrival time at nursery much more peaceful, quiet and calm.

Who was involved?

All the children who were present in the morning session were involved and all the morning staff too.

What did we do?

The doors of the two playrooms were left open and, for example, floor toys were placed in one room and table activities in the other. Some activities were placed in the foyer too, such as jigsaws. In fact the whole nursery was opened up to all the children and staff, apart from the kitchen for safety reasons. The idea was that the children would be able to flow between the activities if they chose to. We were able to supervise the children because the doors were left open and the nursery became open-plan.

What happened as a result?

The children thoroughly enjoyed the freedom of being able to move around the whole nursery, and being able to choose where, what and who they wanted to play with. We noticed that it gave the children the opportunity to play with a variety of activities including self-selection of play materials. It also gave the children opportunity to play with their older and younger peers and in some cases their brothers or sisters. We observed younger children watching the older ones and learning from them by copying their actions.

What was the impact and why?

The 'early morning experimental period' had a considerable impact upon the entire nursery. The children no longer felt cramped, which had caused frustration and led to antagonistic behaviour. They had fewer arguments. The staff in turn felt calm, peaceful and serene because the children were happier. By setting off on a good footing the whole nursery day progressed much more calmly.

2   Increased Autonomy

In the daily planning of the activities the staff wanted to incorporate provision for the development of the children's Autonomy and Initiative. The owner had carried out in-service training to guide the staff into areas that could support children's Autonomy, such as children being allowed to choose their own activities and adults following child-initiated ideas. It was clear from the second

Implementation of the Action Plan: the early morning experimental period. Older children play together with their younger peers and siblings as a consequence of the restructure

round of observations, carried out six months after the Evaluation Stage, that there was a considerable change in the amount of Autonomy that the staff provided for the children in the nursery. These observations were substantiated by the Adult Engagement Scale data. The main developments to be seen were as follows.

- More provision for the children's ideas and their judgment of the end product. Before, the adults had been more restrictive about children finishing an activity when they chose. After the action, the children were allowed time to finish an activity, or could continue it later.

- Children were allowed more freedom of choice in selecting activities and also in terms of adults supporting child-initiated activities. On one occasion the Support Worker observed one member of staff who had set up an activity where the children were cutting up old birthday cards and then making their own collage picture. One child, Lucy, decided to make her collage into a hat but she struggled to make the paper hold fast with glue. The adult watched her for a while and then suggested to Lucy that a few staples may hold better. Lucy agreed and the adult fetched a stapler and helped Lucy to staple her hat. Lucy was justly proud of her hat, and many other children started to make hats too. The adult had supported the child's lead and the activity had become child-initiated.

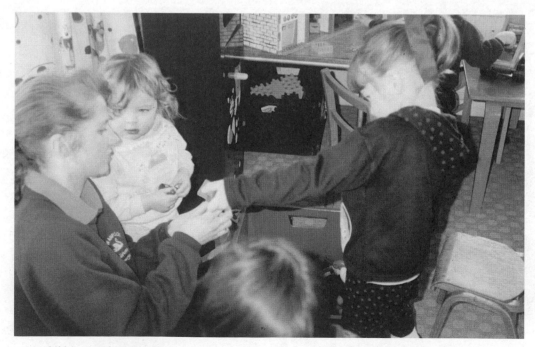

Supporting child-initiated activities

- The area of conflict solving and rules revealed considerable development. The staff helped the children to negotiate solutions to their conflicts rather than as one child stated in an interview, 'J. poked me in the eye – B. (a staff member) put it right'. There was more explanation of the rules so that children could understand why they are important.

- The greatest development could be seen in the staff's handling of behaviour. The staff corrected the action rather than the child and provided wonderfully clear explanations too.

3   More physical activities

The nursery timetable and physical layout of the room was modified to ensure that there was provision for physical, fine motor skills and gross motor skills. The children were given opportunity in the afternoons, if the weather was inclement, to carry out physical exercise such as trampoline, and music and movement.

4   Improved parental communication

In order to better inform the parents of staff movements, roles and qualifications, it was agreed between the parents and the staff that a noticeboard would be placed in the foyer of the nursery incorporating photographs of the current staff. A nursery parent offered to do the artwork which was welcomed by the owner.

REFLECTION ON ACTION

The owner of the setting stated that the project had made her 'sit back and look' at the nursery and it had made her realise that she had,

> got into a rut. It has made me consider the overall nursery and consequently change several practices. One particular change (the increased autonomy) has improved the whole atmosphere in the nursery.

Although the owner had chosen to show the parents the Evaluation Report, she had found it very difficult to do so, as she stated, 'I found it hard involving the parents – but it worked!'

She was very pleased with the restructuring of the early morning, although she knew that some of the established staff had to adapt to the so-called 'lack of structure' that it presented for them. Some of these staff also found it difficult to cope with children having more Autonomy in the nursery, particularly when they could choose their own activities. The staff all found the Child Involvement observations very useful and are continuing to actively use these in the nursery. The parents were pleased to be involved in the process particularly in the interviews and in the reading of the Evaluation Report.

The main purpose of the EEL Evaluation and Development process is for the action to have a positive impact upon practice, practitioners and, ultimately, on the effective learning of young children. One method of recording this effectiveness is through an analysis of the children's Involvement levels. It was clear that the children were experiencing higher levels of Involvement in the nursery when compared to those observed at the beginning of the process. The average level of Involvement was 3.53 for the nursery and this had increased substantially to 3.88. There was also clear evidence that the incidence of level 1 (low) involvement had declined. More children were also experiencing level 5 (high) involvement – the percentage increased from 25 per cent at the beginning of the process to 42 per cent at the end. This is real evidence of successful improvement.

ISSUES FOR FURTHER REFLECTION

This Case Study describes how a team of practitioners in a small private day nursery collaborated with an EEL Support Worker in a process of evaluation and improvement. Their evaluation led them to focus their development on:

- more observation by adults

- giving the children more choice and Autonomy

- providing more physical activity

- giving more information to parents.

The processes they went through in achieving this improvement in their practice raise a number of important questions for discussion by those who work both within this type of setting and beyond.

1   In what ways does an all-day care setting need to differ from part-time provision?

2   Are qualifications/training necessary for practitioners/adults who work with young children?

3   The benefits of working closely with an 'outside critical friend' are evident in this nursery. Could the staff have been more fully involved in the evaluation process?

4   This setting attempted to develop their practice in four areas. Do you agree with their priorities? Did they try to do too much at once?

5   The staff in this nursery were very excited by the observations of children. What does this tell you?

6   What are the difficulties with giving children more Autonomy and choice? What are the benefits?

7   Children's physical development is often under-supported in nurseries. Why is this?

8   The staff in this nursery shared their evaluations directly with the parents. Is this desirable? What are the implications of doing so?

8 Case Study Eight – A Workplace Nursery

Sarah Kelly

Context

This Case Study describes how a team of practitioners at the workplace nursery of a large media organisation, with the children, their parents, and the EEL Support Worker, worked together to build on existing good practice and develop it, and to broaden the range of high quality educational opportunities offered.

The nursery opened six years ago, and was registered for up to 20 pre-school children from four months to school age, each of whom had at least one parent employed by the organisation. At the time of the study six of these children were aged between 3 and 4 years, but this varied from year to year. Children generally attended full-time, from 9.00 am to 6.00 pm, although there were also facilities for part-time children to share a full-time place. The nursery was open all year around but closed to the children for a week in May for maintenance, when the equipment was overhauled and the nursery repainted. The Manager, her Deputy and her three full-time staff were all NNEB qualified Nursery Nurses and there was also a part-time general assistant.

Physical environment

The nursery was situated away from the main organisational complex, in a well-converted sports pavilion. Because of its isolated position among trees it was completely surrounded by a security fence and linked to the main security system. The layout inside was open and spacious with bright, airy rooms for the older and younger children and well-presented, colourful wall and table displays reflecting current themes or children's work. There was a wide variety of good quality educational toys for indoor and outdoor play, to support the whole age range. The room where the 3 and 4 year olds spent much of their day was divided into areas – a well-equipped home corner with dressing-up clothes, a book corner with television, tables and chairs, large toys, a sand tray and more recently a computer. Small equipment was stored on trolleys and in cupboards.

Painting easels, the water tray and other large equipment were brought out occasionally. Because of the wide age and developmental range of children using the room for parts of the day, much of the equipment was not immediately available to the older children.

Nursery organisation

The daily timetable provided opportunity for free and directed play activities within sessions, times for outdoor play and also regular outings. Clear routines were seen as an important aspect of the children's learning, particularly in view of the wide age range. The staff had an excellent working relationship as a team, and together provided a good mixture of high quality care with education. The atmosphere was informal, with staff and parents on first-name terms, but equally was highly organised and professional. They had successfully created a happy, secure and stimulating environment for the children, with the warm atmosphere of an extended family.

Staff spend time talking to the children throughout the day

STRATEGIES FOR WORKING TOGETHER

After the Manager of the nursery had agreed that she and her staff would participate an initial meeting was set up between the Director of the Project, the EEL Support Worker and the staff. This meeting outlined the commitment necessary to cover the Project's four stages of Evaluation, Action Planning, Development and Reflection. The role of the EEL Support Worker was to gather information, but also to support and involve the staff throughout the process. One of the problems for a small, day care setting is that of staff release, so each stage of the Project had to be introduced to staff either individually, in small groups or through the Manager. However, the relatively small numbers of children, staff and parents involved meant that there was time for informal comment and discussion of each stage. As an outsider the Support Worker may be seen to provide a more objective view of a setting – 'to see the setting with new eyes' – as well as taking pressure off the already hardworking staff. On the other hand, having to cope with an outsider's observations is potentially stressful for the staff and, perhaps more importantly, gives the staff less opportunity for working through the Project themselves as a team, coming to grips with it and seeing it as their own. The Support Worker felt that she needed a number of visits to get to know the children and staff, to get a feel for the nursery, the organisation and routine of the day and the relationships between staff, children and parents. This, in turn, gave them a chance to get to know her, and to begin to familiarise themselves with the Project.

EVALUATING PRACTICE

A timetable for the Evaluation Stage of the Project was agreed with the Manager. This included filling in proforma and professional biography forms for the staff, taking photographs, arranging dates for interviewing parents, staff and children, and allocating time for the Child Tracking observations, Child Involvement observations and Adult Engagement observations. The observation schedules focused on:

1   The range of children's activities, their interactions with other children and staff and their level of choice throughout the day (Child Tracking);
2   The children's involvement in their activities (Child Involvement Scale);
3   The adults' relationships with the children, looking specifically at the areas of Sensitivity, Stimulation and Autonomy (Adult Engagement Scale).

It was important to space the information gathering, explaining one section at a time and yet making the whole process coherent and manageable. Photographs were taken throughout the study in order to capture the children in a wide range of activities. The interview questions had to be phrased to suit the differing needs of the interviewees. Children talked more freely in groups of 3 or 4, with photographs of themselves and the nursery as a prompt. For parents, it was sometimes appropriate just to talk informally about their experiences of the nursery, and then to ask questions that had not been covered. The staff found it helpful to have time to reflect on the questions before being interviewed. The child observation schedules were undertaken in part by the staff themselves, while the Support Worker observed the adults alongside the children, in order to avoid the staff feeling under too much pressure. From all this information an Evaluation Report was compiled, using the EEL 10 dimensions of quality as a framework. The purpose of the Report was to present a current picture of the educational experiences of the 3 and 4 year old children at the nursery. In order to ensure that it was complete and accurate, the staff were given the opportunity to discuss and amend it where necessary.

There had been regular and ongoing discussion from the start of the study, and the staff had already considered ways in which they would like to move forward. There is increasing pressure on private and day care nurseries to show that they are able to provide the same educational facilities as schools are seen to give. The staff wanted to produce written statements about the nursery to give parents more information about their policies and aims for the children. The Evaluation Report provided them with a focus for beginning this process, as well as for developing their practice. The first objective was too look at the curriculum, at the activities and experiences available to the children. The Schools' Council (1981) suggests that the curriculum is 'what each child takes away with them'. In the words of the Rumbold Report (DES 1990), the curriculum can be thought of as the total learning experiences, the concepts, knowledge, understanding, attitudes and skills that a child needs to possess. We know that children learn from everything they experience at this stage, through their play activities, from their relationships with other children and adults, and from values and attitudes embedded in the setting. Their learning is holistic and all areas of learning are interlinked which can make it difficult to categorise the curriculum. However in order to plan and to provide appropriate experiences for the child's all-round development, the curriculum was looked at in terms of the broad areas of learning and experience outlined in the Rumbold Report, which were widely accepted as essential for young children's learning.

The nursery was well provided with good quality educational toys, books and equipment through which the children can explore and learn, and in the words of the Manager,

> *learning is through play and through communication with other children and adults.*

The observed activities on offer provided a wide range of opportunities to support the children's all-round development. It is often only possible to guess at what a child of this age is learning from an activity, so during the Child Tracking observations an assessment was made of the areas of learning that the child might be experiencing. These observations revealed that there was quite an imbalance between the areas of experience, with a high incidence of language and human/social experiences and with mathematical, scientific and physical experiences much lower. There may of course be explanations for these results. The sample was limited and the children may well have been engaged in some of these activities when no observations were taking place. Also children were not free to move between the outside and inside because of the wide age range and because of supervision difficulties. But the results gave staff the opportunity to look closely at the equipment and opportunities being provided for the children, and at the way in which they were being used. Subsequently, in the Action Plan, the staff tried to find ways in which to address the apparent imbalances in the areas of learning.

Using the Child Involvement Scale is one way of measuring the quality of children's learning experiences. It is likely that learning is taking place if they:

- are fully engaged with their activity

- are persisting and concentrating very well

- cannot be distracted and show energy, purpose and enthusiasm.

Involvement was measured on a scale of 1 to 5, and observations of the children showed that levels of Involvement were generally high, but variable, particularly in the morning. The degree of Involvement varied widely within the two-minute observations and the children appeared to 'flit' from one activity to another. Further information gathered from the Child Tracking observations and from interviews with children gave a more complete picture, as children were not always clear about the things they liked to do. So although levels of Involvement were high, and staff were clearly providing high quality and appropriate learning opportunities for the children, there was scope for helping children to focus more on their own interests. Children appeared to

At the hairdresser's – a plastic fork makes a wonderful comb

settle down as the day went on, and after lunch often played long and involved games in and out of the home corner, transforming it into a hospital, hairdresser's or the base for a journey, using dressing-up clothes and other toys as props. These games would spill into the whole room and often included the younger children as well as the staff.

The Child Tracking observations record an individual's activities throughout the day, and the amount of choice a child has in choosing activities. This choice was recorded on a scale of 1 to 4; at level 1 the child is obliged to do the activity, while at level 4 complete freedom of choice is given. Observations showed that, in general, the choice was more limited in the mornings (level 2) when activities were chosen by staff, and although children were free to ask for anything they wanted, they didn't tend to do so. They often played alone or with another child, unless they were working with an adult on a structured art or craft activity. In the afternoon children were normally asked to choose what they would like to do (level 3), and adults often became more involved in their imaginary play, table-top games or preschool activities. Children were observed

Creating space and time for talk between adults and children

to become more settled and more involved with their activities at this time of day with adults intervening to develop their play.

The quality of children's learning experiences was affected by the role and attitude of the staff in the setting, and by their sensitivity to the children's needs. Staff believed, first and foremost, that they should provide a safe and secure environment for the children, and one in which each child could develop as an individual with support and encouragement from all the staff. Social and emotional wellbeing, confidence building and self-esteem were seen to be very important. Parents were full of praise for the genuine care and affection shown to the children so that they were happy and settled. Great emphasis was placed on communication between staff and children, as well as between staff and parents. The staff believed that 'they should talk about things, show by example and encourage questioning', while a parent's view of the teaching style was that it was 'not forced or pressured, but encouraged where necessary'.

The small numbers of children and high staff ratios at the nursery meant that there was space and time for individuals.

The Adult Engagement Scale looked at three categories of adult behaviour which were believed to be critical in the effectiveness of the learning experience: Sensitivity, Stimulation and Autonomy. The results of the observations showed that the staff were very sensitive to children's emotional wellbeing and sincere and responsive to their needs. They were communicating well with children, talking and explaining things to them. Staff were less active in giving children opportunities for experimentation, using their own ideas and for making their own decisions and choices. Looked at in conjunction with the Child Tracking and Child Involvement observations, these results seemed to show that the most successful learning experiences were those in which children were able to choose their own activities, but where adults became involved to extend and to develop their interests. It is important to note that in order to broaden children's experiences, it was not necessary, or indeed desirable, to provide more formal learning opportunities in particular areas. From the observations it seemed to be much more valuable for adults to interact and to extend play activities to widen the children's experiences and opportunities.

Action Planning

When the Evaluation Report had been completed, a meeting was held with the Manager and Deputy to discuss the findings and to decide priorities for action. This was subsequently shared with the rest of the staff with the aim of drawing up an Action Plan. The Action Plan involved the staff in looking more closely at the curriculum, particularly with regard to the apparent imbalance between the areas of learning. From there they planned to develop a curriculum policy covering the range of opportunities offered to the children. This had a two-fold purpose: firstly, to focus for themselves on the range and balance of the learning experiences offered to the children, and secondly, to provide information for parents. Parents had close contact with the nursery on a twice-daily basis and were encouraged to exchange information about their child. They were very appreciative of the amount of contact given in general, but expressed the need to have more feedback about children's learning activities so that they could follow up interests at home and practise skills where necessary. The staff were concerned that parents did not know what their children had been doing during the day, and that there was not always time or opportunity to tell them. They considered extending the daily diary scheme, kept at present for the babies, to include the older children as well. They believed that this would give parents more information and the opportunity to become more involved in their children's learning. At the same time they began to display more information for parents, including topic plans showing areas of learning and activities to be covered.

IMPROVING PRACTICE

In drawing up their policies, the staff referred to a number of publications including *Aspects of Primary Education, the Education of Children under Five* (DES 1989), Starting with Quality (the Rumbold Report) (DES 1990) and a number of County Education Policies for Under-5s. Their Action Plan also included making contact with other local nurseries and the local university crèche. Staff in small day care settings face particular difficulties in that they are generally not able to be released for meetings and courses and may feel very isolated. Contact is important for providing mutual support and for the exchange of information, in particular educational information which is not always freely available outside the education service. The staff discussed making contact with local authority nursery schools in order to share information on curriculum development, and they noted that there were plans within the local authority to develop and integrate services for young children which might facilitate this in the future.

Three months after the Action Plan had been put in operation, the Final Report described the action that had already been undertaken. A curriculum policy had been formulated and more discussion and planning was taking place. The aims of the nursery had been written and displayed in the entrance hall. The staff had visited a number of other local nurseries, and planned that these visits should be reciprocal and ongoing. In addition they were in the process of implementing a daily record sheet for each child for which they had already received positive feedback from parents.

REFLECTION ON ACTION

From the final Project feedback it was evident that staff valued the more positive approach they were developing with parents, as well as the greater understanding they had gained of the children's needs and how best to respond to them. Whilst they acknowledged the difficulties of having an outsider working with them and observing them, staff valued the outside perspective they had been given. They felt it had helped them to understand and discuss new developments to improve their organisation and practice. By linking with other nurseries they should now be able to continue improving good practice and to broaden the educational opportunities for the children.

Issues For Further Reflection

This Case Study described how a team of workers in a small workplace nursery collaborated with an EEL Support Worker to evaluate the quality of their provision and to develop an Action Plan for improvement. The focus of their action was:

- developing the range of learning experiences offered;

- giving the children more choice and Autonomy;

- providing parents with more information.

The processes they went through in achieving this improvement in their practice raise a number of important questions for discussion by those who work both within this type of setting and beyond.

1   What were the issues facing the outside EEL Support Worker within this setting? How did she tackle these?
2   What should the curriculum priorities be for 3 and 4 year olds? How might they be developed in a nursery with little access to trained educational advisers?
3   What are the advantages and challenges of working in a nursery with children from birth to 5 years?
4   What strategies may be used to increase children's Autonomy within a nursery? What effects will this have?
5   How do we enhance parental partnership in a nursery where all parents work?
6   What are the particular issues for developing staff in the private sector? How might these be tackled?
7   Where might the practitioners in this private sector nursery go for help and support in their development?
8   What are the benefits for a workplace nursery of embarking on an evaluation and improvement process? What are the difficulties?

9 Case Study Nine – A Primary School Reception Class

Tony Bertram

Context

This setting was a large, two-form entry Junior and Infant School for children aged 4 to 11 years of age. It was housed in premises built in the 1970s, during a period of urban renewal and redevelopment in the inner-city area of a large urban conurbation. There were more than 400 children on roll, with a male headteacher and a staff of 14, who were mostly women. In addition there was a part time (0.5) home/school liaison teacher. The catchment area included several older streets of terraced houses built towards the end of the Victorian era to accommodate industrial workers. The immediate area around the school was council-owned property, dating from the more recent urban renewal strategies of the 1970–80s.

The majority of children qualified for free school meals indicating that most families did not have a wage earner or were on Family Income Support. The ethnic origins of the children's families were Pakistani 59 per cent, Afro-Caribbean 10 per cent, Indian 9 per cent, Bangladesh 7 per cent, British 7 per cent, Arab 6 per cent, other 2 per cent. English was the first choice home language for only 8 per cent of the families. Most children lived in stable two-parent families with extended links to wider family and community support. There was a relatively high turnover of pupils: new arrivals and leavers made up just over 10 per cent of the total number on roll. Most of the new arrivals had no English. Some children were away for an extended period over the summer to visit relatives abroad.

The physical environment

The Reception Unit was in a wing on the lower ground floor which made it distinct but not separate from the main building. There were 48 children in this Unit which was divided into two reception classes. The classes were linked by an external corridor which ran down one side of the rooms. The corridor was sometimes used for activities and at the end of it was a small room which could

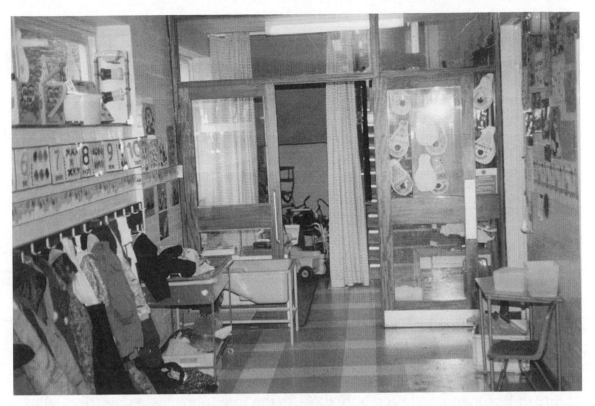

The corridor used for play activities

sometimes be used for interviews with parents or for withdrawing children for special attention. For almost 10 years the LEA had admitted a year cohort of children in the September following their 4th birthday. In May, when the EEL Project was carried out, approximately 25 per cent of the children in the two classes were still under the age of 5. Most of the children had previously attended a Nursery Centre part-time.

The children attended the reception class from 08.55 am until 3.30 pm, with a lunch break from 12.00–1.25, and most of them stayed for lunch. They had no separate outside area in which to play during breaks and they attended whole-school assemblies on alternate days, with a smaller assembly for the Key Stage 1 classes on the other days. They made use of the two halls in the main building for PE and dinners and they could also use a local sports centre once a week.

Staffing

Staffing for the two reception classes consisted of two, full-time certificated teachers and a full-time classroom assistant, who spoke English, Punjabi and

Urdu. There were also two part-time assistants, who were shared with other classes. The headteacher had overall responsibility for the school and the budget had been fully delegated from the LEA for over a year. The Chair of Governors was a member of the British Asian community and the school worked hard at its relationships with the parents.

STRATEGIES FOR WORKING TOGETHER

This study focused on only one of the reception classes because of logistical issues and the developmental nature of the Project at this stage. The teacher of this class had overall responsibility for the Early Years and Music and was also Co-ordinator for Key Stage 1, that is, for the six classes included between Year R and Year 2. The staff in both reception classes, including the teachers and ancillary helpers, were informed about the methodology and observation techniques of the EEL Project, but the EEL Support Worker operated only in the Co-ordinator's classroom. Meetings were held regularly with the head, who was included in the interviews and invited to comment on the Evaluation Report and the Action Plan. Although other members of the school staff were aware of the ongoing Project, only those in the reception classes contributed to the Evaluation process and only one classroom practice was observed in detail. All the reception staff were invited to participate in, contribute to and critique the methodology and the documentary outcomes of the evaluation.

In the past children were assigned to the two reception classes on the basis of chronological age, so that one contained older and the other younger children. However, this had recently changed and the classes were now equally balanced. This, it was thought, allowed more opportunity for joint planning between the teachers of the two classes, although as one said,

> We decide together what we are going to do but what actually happens in the classroom is all me!

Both teachers in the reception classes were highly experienced, having more than 56 years of working with young children between them, but they felt this was sometimes not acknowledged. One ancillary had been educated in east Africa and spoke Punjabi and Urdu as well as English. She had been at the school for 14 years. The NNEB had worked for 19 years with 'under school-aged children', a phrase that reflected some of her concerns about early formal schooling. The staff suggested that recent changes, mostly emanating from outside the school, had left them less sure about their abilities and they worried

The ancillary working with a group of children

that they were often being asked to do things which they felt were not suited to the needs of their children. They were losing confidence, and their commitment to the system – although not to their children – had become increasingly doubtful. One of the teachers said she would like to retire and come back to work alongside whoever replaced her. She felt that this would allow her to have access to the children but without the responsibility for doing things which she thought were inappropriate for these very young children.

These tensions came mainly from what one teacher described as the 'hidden pressure of the National Curriculum'. Although their 4 year old children were not part of the statutory provision there was an almost unspoken understanding that the management of the school perceived the 'real business' of the reception class to be predominantly cognitive development, and that even this should be narrowed more prescriptively to focus on National Curriculum objectives. Yet the documentation of the school offered a wider view of its aims. The school prospectus, whilst acknowledging that 'the requirements of the National Curriculum are fully met', listed such things as 'encouraging self-esteem, emotional and social development, responsiveness to others, developing positive attitudes'. The Governors' curriculum statement also declared a wider view of the curriculum which should include 'the other aspects of a child's development – social, physical, emotional'. The reality of what the reception teachers felt they were being asked to do contrasted with the rhetoric of the public statements. These experienced reception teachers were more interested in inculcating and encouraging dispositions to learning – enthusiasm, curiosity, persistence, creativity, precision, interest – than, as they saw it, switching those things off in their eager-to-learn children by introducing a formal, prescriptive curriculum too early. They were also more conscious of the emotional wellbeing of the children and the social context of their learning. These differing perceptions of the needs of their children were at the root of the tensions between the early years staff and the school management.

The reception teacher's views was that she wanted her children:

> to be happy, to enjoy coming to school and to learn. If I have the first two of these, I can ensure the third.

The tension between a child-centred, individualised, active curriculum encouraging exploration and experience, and the requirements of the National Curriculum with its emphasis on entitlement to a common core of knowledge, teacher centredness and delivery, was most acute in this first year of schooling. The headteacher was sensitive to this but had a hard-nosed pragmatism:

> There is such a lot in Key Stage 1. Four year olds are a different kettle of fish. In the nursery they enjoyed a staff ratio of 1:13. They were geared for play. It is difficult for them to adjust. We need to build on what they've had but there are big changes for them. They mix with Y6 on the playground. Whatever time they came in there'd be a big jump, so they might as well get used to it from day one.

These tensions between management and reception about what was considered to be appropriate practice were further complicated by considerations about appropriate staffing. Clearly staffing was a key ingredient in deciding how the curriculum could be implemented. Larger ratios were forcing the reception staff to spend less time with individuals or small groups. These debates often became focused on the amount of ancillary help available to the early years teachers. The headteacher said:

> When we first admitted 4 year olds the LEA said that we had to have classroom assistants working alongside the teacher. We are in charge of our own budget now and we have compromised. We don't use 100 per cent of their time with reception,

though it is virtually. Guided play needs adults there to harness it, use and extend it. Play should be part of the curriculum down there. But it's a question of balance with your staffing. The more you can put in down there, the less likely you are to get problems later but I've got to think of the whole school. The emphasis needs to be on the reception class but I have to acknowledge that help is also required higher up.

The difference between the head's and the teachers' perception of this issue caused some tensions.

There's me and the part-time ancillaries, one trained and one untrained. I'm quite a lot on my own, perhaps about half the time. I do have Mums in. I did have two regulars but the best ones tend to get jobs and move on. Just going to the Sports Centre, I need 5 adults to help cross the roads. They gradually drop out. I have control of the class but to change the effectiveness of the children's learning I need trained, valuable support staff.

My role is first and foremost a class teacher. I'd like to get on with the job in hand without bureaucratic interference, I'd like teachers to be consulted and expertise recognised. I'd like more recognition that early years teaching is important for the development of the whole child and that we need more and suitable resourcing. I'd like more bilingual help and more chances to liaise with feeder nurseries and parents.

The parents had a view about the staffing especially as they compared it with the children's previous experience in the Nursery Centre. One commented,

There are too many children for one teacher. These children need attention and not to be left out.

The reception staff were keen to become better at their job. They were mature and experienced but they were still eager to be made aware of new developments and research. They also felt that they would like to have more professional development in areas other than curriculum subjects and assessment. They felt nonteaching staff should also have access to staff development courses.

EVALUATING PRACTICE

The EEL Project allowed these concerns to be aired and documented objectively. The structured interviews provided an opportunity for all the participants' views to be expressed democratically and written down in the Evaluation Report. This at least allowed the head and the staff to see their differing perspectives and to become aware of some of the parents' perspectives.

Observational evidence from the Child Involvement and Adult Engagement Scales was able to show that different patterns were discernible in both the children's and the adults' behaviour when there was a change in the adult:pupil ratios. Children displayed higher levels of Involvement in their activities when there were more adults available to support their learning and interact with them. The adults' style of teaching changed with variations in pupil:adult ratio. The adults scored higher on their ability to give the children Autonomy when there were lower ratios of children to adults. Differences in the overall level of

Children involved in a range of different activities during an afternoon session

children's Involvement were noted between morning and afternoon sessions. Children became more involved in the afternoon sessions, when they were allowed more freedom and choice. Morning sessions tended to be teacher-centred and more formal. More talk, both in English and home language, was observed in the greater number of interactions which characterised the afternoon sessions. Thus research evidence was obtained, systematically and rigorously, on which judgments could be made about taking practice forward. The observational evidence allowed a diagnostic assessment of the situation.

ACTION PLANNING

Having made an evaluation of the practice within the classroom, all the participants had an opportunity to review the provisional Report and comment, looking for inaccuracies or disagreements, so that the written Evaluation Report could be said to incorporate all their viewpoints and the research evidence. These minor adjustments ensured that there was a degree of agreement in that this Report captured the strengths and the weaknesses of the setting in relation to its provision for 4 year old children. The Report was circulated and staff and the headteacher were asked to attend an Action Planning meeting where the Evaluation Report would be discussed. Each person was asked to bring two lists, one which itemised achievements that they thought should be celebrated and one which identified where improvements might be made. The lists were collated and, where possible, combined and they gave rise to a thorough debate. Following this, a decision was made to try to prioritise the list of areas for improvement and this eventually formed the Action Plan.

The issues which emerged highlighted the following needs:

- to introduce more Autonomy and choice into the curriculum and ensure more balance in the teaching strategies between morning and afternoon sessions;

- more play and talk and for the curriculum to be developmentally appropriate;

- greater preschool liaison with feeder providers, home visits to parents and for a written policy on the induction and admission of children;

- consistency in the school's parental help policy;

- more opportunities for outside play with direct access and suitable equipment, and either a separated place or a separated time from the whole-school playground;

- more storage space and resources;
- additional staffing and the reception class size to be kept low.

After discussion it was agreed that the central aim of the Action Plan would be to facilitate more small groupwork and achieve an active, play-orientated curriculum appropriate to the developmental level of these nursery-aged children.

The Action Plan contained four strategies:

1   to review the classroom layout and develop space and resources for play;
2   to modify and develop the curriculum planning procedures to include opportunities for children to be more involved in making decisions about their programme of learning and for more use of play;
3   to review classroom organisational strategies to allow for more choice and Autonomy by children;
4   to develop the outdoor area as an adjunct to the classroom.

IMPROVING PRACTICE

During the following five months the reception staff met and considered how they approached 'set activities', that is, activities that the children had to experience. They looked at how these might be appropriately learned through play experiences. They attempted to involve the children more in the planning of their day and introduced elements of choice. Parents were asked to become involved in planning and evaluating through wall displays in the areas where they congregated while waiting, which invited participation. Children took home 'Ask me about . . .' slips on which the teacher had written an event that had happened to a child during the day. These provided a focus for discussion between child and parent. The children were also encouraged to regularly review and evaluate their learning and to share this with their peers in circle sessions. A timescale for each step in the Action Plan was written down and responsibilities for each staff member were delineated.

The initial cycle of evaluation and development took 10 months. This confirmed that one of the real strengths of the reception staff was their openness to opportunities for their professional development at a time of constant change and pressure from policy initiatives at local and national level. This initiative took place during a period of sustained pressure within the school. To some extent the concerns expressed by the headteacher regarding difficulties over funding were confirmed, but some of the problems relating to storage of equipment in the classrooms, and children's ease of access to it, were addressed and more space was thus created. The development of a separate play area for the reception children, however, would have to await further resourcing.

The increased involvement of parents was partially successful. A bulletin board was set up, comment books were passed between home and school and the 'Ask me about . . .' slips had also increased parents' awareness of the many curriculum activities which their children enjoyed. Staff were keen to get extra resourcing to support their understanding of the multiethnic and multilanguage issues but again there were not sufficient reserves to sustain this.

Classroom layouts were changed to be more conducive to active, experiential learning and space was developed to allow for more play and choice. A pictorial proforma was designed that enabled the children to indicate how they intended to plan their day and was also used to help the children assess how far they had achieved their aims. Play was given more priority in planning but the adults also ensured that they participated more in the children's play, sometimes extending, guiding, observing, intervening, directing and sometimes supporting or enhancing language development, and always being sensitive to the child's needs. The staff, having been made aware of the Child Involvement Scale, were much more focused on systematic observation of the children.

REFLECTION ON ACTION

All the staff expressed a belief in giving more choice and Autonomy to the children but said that they had felt pressured to do otherwise by the demands of the National Curriculum. Their new classroom organisational strategies enabled this to happen. They now allowed children to decide *when* they would do activities, *who* they might do the activities with and allowed them to plan *how* they might do some activities themselves. Observations by the EEL Support Worker revealed the children making genuine choices about their activities. Within limits they now had a much greater range of opportunities for choice. Staff encouraged the children to interpret and express their ideas, to make choices and experiment. There was more negotiation and less conflict. The needs of the National Curriculum were balanced with the needs of the individual child. Choice was fostered, respected and supported. Children who found choice difficult were helped and teachers reported that children got better at making informed choices with experience. The quality of their learning was enhanced by the increased motivation which accompanied this growing independence and Autonomy. The staff at times expressed surprise at what the children were capable of achieving, and they themselves became more confident in giving responsibility to the children. These impressions were substantiated when the key research instruments were reapplied.

The Involvement levels of the children were measurably higher when the second schedule of observation scales was implemented by the EEL Support Worker towards the end of the Development Stage. Further, although Involvement scores for all the children increased, the greatest increase was amongst the youngest children and amongst boys.

Despite allowing for more Autonomy, there was a significant increase in the number of interactions between children and adults and in their quality. The staff interventions were more open-ended and children had far more choice of activity and responsibility. Children were more confident and expressed themselves more. The dialogue had become much less adult-directed. Children were asking more questions and initiating dialogue. Teachers were doing more scaffolding and enabling, and were less in didactic mode.

There were thus measurable changes in the school's provision for its 4 year olds over these two terms and most, if not all, of the Action Plan was achieved. The staff were stronger in their beliefs and better able to articulate them. They were able to point to a systematic and rigorous framework of evaluation which made them more certain of their genuine achievements and able to measure the success of new initiatives. They felt in charge of this process and empowered by it. They had a new focus on developing quality and it was internally driven. Furthermore this was perceived as only the end of an initial cycle. Their next cycle would begin by refocusing on those issues which they had highlighted in their original evaluation but not prioritised: firstly, to address the need for greater preschool liaison with feeder providers, for home visits and for a written policy on admission and induction procedures; secondly, to develop the outdoor play area adjacent to the classroom; and thirdly, to extend and develop the existing links with parents.

A great deal was achieved during the 10-month process and it was clear that the work would continue. The cycle of evaluation and improvement is something that the staff are committed to and have made their own. They should be congratulated on their professionalism and dedication. Most staff want to improve the quality of their teaching and the learning of their children. The EEL Project gave this setting the framework to do so.

ISSUES FOR FURTHER REFLECTION

This Case Study describes how a small team of teachers and ancillary workers in a Reception Unit of a large primary school collaborated with an EEL Support Worker to gather evidence about the quality of their provision and to develop a strategy to enhance it. Their attention focused on:

- providing a more play-oriented curriculum and environment;

- giving the children more choice and Autonomy.

The processes they went through in achieving this improvement in their practice raise a number of important questions for discussion by those who work both within this type of setting and beyond.

1   How inclusive should the evaluative process be? Who should be involved in a large school organisation? Is it harder for reception class staff to undertake the evaluative processes themselves? Why?

2   How might reception class staff respond to the downward pressures of the National Curriculum?

3   What learning experiences should a reception class provide? What are the priorities and why?

4   These reception class teachers did not have full-time ancillary support. How important are staffing ratios to the quality of learning offered?

5   How should the day be structured in a full-time reception class? Should morning and afternoon sessions be different?

6   How much choice and Autonomy are 4 year olds capable of handling? What are the factors to consider here?

7   How do reception teachers balance the need for an active, play-oriented curriculum with the perceived demands of the National Curriculum, in which they are caught?

8   How important is outside play to reception children? What might the staff have done to ensure access to this?

9   Senior management staff in primary schools sometimes need educating in the needs of young children. How might this be tackled?

10 REFLECTIONS AND EMERGING ISSUES

Christine Pascal and Tony Bertram

WHAT WE HAVE LEARNED ABOUT EVALUATION AND IMPROVEMENT

The EEL Project has taught us much about evaluative processes and their potential for improving the quality of provision for young children. More than anything else it has deepened our respect for the professionalism and commitment of those who work with young children. It has also provided us with some clear indications of how high quality and effective early learning may be achieved in the UK. Although we are still at an early stage in our reflections on the process of evaluation there are some tangible issues deserving further consideration which emerge from these Case Studies of EEL in action.

1 Evaluation and improvement is possible and desired in all settings

We have been impressed by the energy that all the EEL Project practitioners have displayed in their commitment to improving the practice and the quality of early learning they offer. All sectors and providers expressed a great desire to develop their knowledge and expertise and were very open to evaluative strategies which would facilitate this. We had participants from all areas of the early childhood world and everyone was excited and positive at the prospect of working together to evaluate and improve their provision. In fact, there was much goodwill and desire to work across the sectors in a multiprofessional way which has resulted in different providers in a local area networking and supporting each other.

   In all the settings we have worked, we have documented clear and identifiable changes in practice. These changes cover many different aspects of practice, from the physical environment, the curriculum, relationships with parents, organisation to developing the role of play in learning. Improvements in the quality of the early learning experiences offered can be claimed in all settings that have completed the cycle of 'evaluation and development'. This is very strong evidence of the power of evaluative processes as a vehicle for change.

2   A democratic approach is effective but requires some external support

In the EEL Project we have tried to ensure that quality is defined by the shared reflections and agreement of experienced managers, practitioners, parents and children. The definition is validated and scrutinised for accuracy by those closest to the experience that is being evaluated. The Project is therefore firmly founded in democratic principles and we have worked hard at putting into place a process which depends on partnership, collaboration and teamwork. Other UK quality evaluation initiatives have adopted a similar inclusive, collaborative approach (the PLA Accreditation Scheme 1993 and the Strathclyde Project 1992). Others have tended to view the process as being more effectively carried out by an external team of 'experts' who come into an early childhood setting and implement the quality evaluation process (the British Standards Scheme 1991 and the OFSTED Inspection Scheme 1993, 1996). However, we believe that if ongoing quality evaluation is viewed as part of a complex set of continuously evolving relationships between providers, children and their families, then it is crucial that approaches adopt a participative, collaborative mode of operation. For us, this is a key issue to be addressed by those concerned with developing quality. We have found that parents, children and practitioners need to be encouraged to work in a mutually open, honest and supportive partnership which is directed towards ensuring the highest quality of early learning experiences possible.

3   Evaluation and improvement should go hand in hand

We are convinced that quality evaluation, inspection or accreditation should not be separated from the development process. It also appears helpful if those who evaluate quality are also involved in the improvement process. The need for continuity and for the extended dialogue that accompanies and follows on from the evaluation process must be facilitated. Those who evaluate quality need to feed in to the development process.

It has also become clear that self-evaluation and development are less effective than externally validated self-evaluation and development. Staff needed the support, advice and encouragement of an outside perspective to develop. The staff found the democratic approach, in which all practitioners were involved, attractive, as it gave them a feeling of self-worth and professional responsibility. Yet, they all indicated that the outside support was critically important at key points in the Evaluation process. The level of this support varied according to the setting and the issues they chose to tackle. We felt this was appropriate as some settings were more developed than others with staff more used to handling the kind of process we were taking them through. There was a consensus of opinion, however, that whether or not the setting was providing high quality, all of them needed to continue to develop and an external source of new knowledge and opinion was invaluable.

4   The evaluative framework used must be rigorous but flexible

There are three issues which need careful consideration in developing evaluative frameworks. Firstly, to be effective any evaluative framework must be rigorous, systematic and based upon the best knowledge we have about effective teaching and learning in the early years. This will involve the development and utilisation of accessible and practicable techniques for gathering and analysing evidence on which to base the evaluation and the training of practitioners in employing them. At the heart of these techniques should be focused observations of adults and children within a setting, but they will also include a range of other qualitative and quantitative methods of gathering information. The model of practitioner as researcher should therefore be viewed as central to the quality improvement process.

Secondly, while the framework itself has to be robust and transferable, it also has to be flexible so that each element within it can be interpreted to meet the particular context in which it is being applied. The diverse range of early childhood settings within the UK, and the need for these to be responsive to the families and local community they serve, has demanded that there is room within any quality framework for it to be applied in different ways. This flexibility should allow individual settings to offer parents real choice whilst reassuring them that the core elements of quality are being addressed.

Thirdly all those participating in the evaluative process must be aware of this quality framework and agree on its validity and applicability to their particular context. Where dispute arises as to the relevance or appropriateness of any aspect of the framework, the effectiveness of the whole process is threatened. The evaluative framework being used must have credibility and acceptance amongst all members of the organisation which is being evaluated.

This requires good communication, time for everyone to familiarise themselves with the framework, and opportunities for an open dialogue about it.

5   The need for time

Experience has also taught us that a dip stick approach to quality evaluation and improvement severely limits its effectiveness. In order to obtain a comprehensive, truly representative and valid picture of the quality of provision in any one setting, which can be used as the basis for fundamental improvement which will have a lasting impact, a long-term timeframe has to be used. The EEL Project's evaluation and improvement process takes between 12 to 15 months to go through just one cycle of focused development. Other schemes also have an extended time period for their implementation, for example the Strathclyde project took over 12 months and the PLA scheme has no time limits. We have found it is important that the process of quality improvement is not viewed as a short, sharp blast of activity which can be done periodically and then put on one side. Rather, we would promote a model of ongoing, professional activity directed at a constantly rolling cycle of evaluation and improvement. In this way short, medium- and longterm goals can be planned for, and worked at systematically, and at a pace which individual settings can manage within the normal ebbs and flows of their activity. We have found this to be not only pragmatic and realistic, but also motivating for those involved because they feel in control.

6   The need for evaluative instruments which assess process as well as outcomes

Evaluating the quality of the processes that go on within any early childhood setting is a very tricky task. It is not easy to identify the constituent elements within a quality experience and to gather 'hard' evidence about changes in these. We are only just beginning to understand the subtle qualitative nuances, interpersonal relationships and factors which constitute effective teaching and learning at this stage, but it is clear that these are the critical factors in determining a quality education or not. As a result of this lack of well-developed techniques, process measures do not seem to carry the same attraction to those who evaluate quality in early childhood. Outcome measures which can provide tangible and often quantifiable evidence are often seen, mistakenly in our view, as preferable. This is despite the fact that the outcomes of educational inputs in these early stages may not be evident until the child reaches maturity.

However, we would be wrong to polarise the debate. It is important that we focus our attention on the development of evaluative instruments which can assess the quality of any early childhood programme. Some of these instruments may focus on educational outcomes and these would include, for example, a child's social competence, emotional wellbeing, behavioural characteristics, linguistic skills, mathematical competencies. However, given the emphasis placed upon learning processes at this stage (DES 1990), we urgently need to develop evaluative instruments which provide reliable and accessible evidence of the quality of these processes. These measures are beginning to emerge and to be utilised within quality improvement schemes. For example, the EEL Project has developed the Child Involvement Scale (Laevers 1994) which focuses on the quality of the learning process and the Adult Engagement Scale (Bertram 1996) which focuses on the quality of the teaching process. These two structured observational techniques are manageable and accessible and have provided invaluable evidence to practitioners, providers and consumers, and may be used diagnostically and evaluatively to monitor developments in quality over time and to make comparisons. More work needs to be done in this important area and also in convincing decisionmakers of the validity and reliability of such process measures. It is interesting to note that amongst the quality schemes currently available to early childhood providers, few are addressing the issue of monitoring the impact of improvements on the quality of teaching and learning at all.

7   The process can result in professional development of practitioners

One of the primary aims of the Project was to use the Evaluation and Improvement process as a cost-effective and targeted process of professional development for the participating practitioners. All participants were trained in the observation and data-gathering process, and shown how to interpret the data and use it for developing an action plan for improvement. The aim was to generate in each study setting a research community and to encourage the practitioners to use their new skills to investigate and review their practice more systematically and rigorously.

Practitioners have reported changes in their thinking and understanding of their practice. In particular, they report that they are observing the learning process more critically and more regularly and using this information to inform their planning. The Project also provided practitioners with a shared set of concepts and vocabulary about learning and teaching, which all of them could use, across the sectors, in dialogues about their work. This rich and rigorous dialogue provides a powerful vehicle for professional and institutional development.

8   The process empowers the practitioners

Part of professional development should be about becoming more confident, having an awareness of practice, having a rationale and being able to articulate this. Evidence is emerging that practitioners who are working with the EEL methodology are empowered by the process. Taking responsibility for evaluating their practice, being given the tools to undertake this, and the means to develop their practice, has given the practitioners a sense of self-worth and control over their professional lives. They report higher self-esteem and a growing belief in the importance and complexity of their work. They are also better able to communicate this to those to whom they are accountable.

We believe that strong and confident practitioners working in an open and self-critical context provide the right conditions for long-term development and change. It is exactly these conditions that the EEL process aims to encourage so that working together for improvement becomes part of the ethos of every early childhood setting.

STRATEGIES FOR SUCCESSFUL EVALUATION AND IMPROVEMENT

All thirteen settings in the first phase of the EEL Project reported a measure of success in their overarching aim of raising the quality of their provision for young children. As the case studies reveal, the shape and form of this improvement varied widely according to the focus of the Action Plan. Reflections on the process have highlighted a number of strategies which appeared to lead to more effective action by the participants. Those who are to embark on this process might find the experience of others who have worked through the EEL Evaluation and Improvement Process helpful.

Hints for success

* **Be open and honest about your intentions.** Share what you are doing with all who might be affected. Try to involve them as far as possible and to keep them fully informed throughout the Evaluation and Improvement process.

- **Don't rush through the process.** Change takes time and it is important that those involved don't feel over-pressurised as resentment will creep in and the development will suffer.

- **Make sure your Action Plan has a clear purpose and focus and that this is explained to all who are affected by it.** Uncertainty and fear about what you might be doing will engender resistance.

- **Be realistic in what you aim to achieve.** It is better to progress step by step. Small victories will fuel larger developments and give participants a sense of achievement. Try to break down your larger scale intentions into prioritised, short-term goals.

- **Be prepared to set aside time and energy for the process.** Success will be limited if this process comes bottom of your list of priorities. If you are not wholly committed to improving the quality of play in your setting it is unlikely that others will be motivated to do so.

- **Be systematic and organised as you progress through the stages.** Data gathering needs equipment, time and organisation. Notification of meetings needs to be given in advance and the venue and format given careful consideration if the meeting is to be productive.

- **Be prepared to act as an advocate for what you believe in.** Convincing others of the rationale for your action is critically important, particularly in the competition over resources. You must be prepared to promote the importance of excellent learning activities in your setting and be absolutely clear about what you need to achieve this. Putting young children's learning on the agenda of all decisionmakers and resource holders is a key to success.

A final piece of advice

An early years adviser gave this final piece of advice for anyone embarking on a process of evaluation and improvement:

> *Be very clear about why you want to do it. Be convinced you are doing it because it is for the benefit of the children first and foremost. If you are not, don't bother because you will never be focused enough in the way that you carry it forward because you won't know why you are doing it. And then go for it, be very well organised, structure it so that you can support your colleagues properly, recognise that they are going to have times of difficulty and be ready to cope with it when they need support. And manage it so that everyone feels they can play a part in shaping it. That would be the advice I would give.*

Some Practitioner Reflections

Discussions with colleagues who have worked on the EEL Project reveal both its strengths and the challenges it offers. Practitioners who have worked on the project were asked to reflect on the process and its impact on the quality of their provision. One team reported that,

> *For a long time we have recognised the need to evaluate and change our provision. The project has enabled us to do this. We have all developed greater insight and awareness of the needs of 4 year olds, and are trying to address this in our daily work. We are very positive about the advantages of the Project, and feel that other people might be able to benefit as we have.*

Many practitioners felt their policies, aims and values were communicated easily to others simply because they were implicit in their practice. One colleague highlighted this in her response.

> *Between members of staff there is an implied understanding but it needs to be developed into a coherent and generally agreed policy. It is obvious that aims and objectives vary between individuals although all would adhere to the assumption of a child-centred curriculum. Policy at present is communicated through classroom practice which is why ambiguities are apparent. Our recent chat sessions for Reception parents and for Governors allowed us to share our philosophy on learning. It was suggested that similar sharing should take place with different year groups.*

In writing down and sharing their views about their practice they had to confront the fact that not everybody shared the same vision and many were mistaken in their assumptions about other colleagues' rationales. This gave rise initially to some difficulties and required tact, compromise and negotiation. It also required a re-examination of beliefs and the confidence to hold them up for scrutiny. Sometimes this meant abandoning or altering long-cherished beliefs. This process became part of the professional development of individuals, making them more articulate about what was central to their view of learning and more positive about its value. The process also brought about a greater understanding of parents' needs and attitudes.

We were pleased to find practitioners through the Project celebrating their successes as well as identifying areas for development. As one practitioner stated,

Through doing the Evaluation schedule, I was able to reflect upon the provision in my nursery. On the whole I was pleased with my findings. I am not smug or self-satisfied because I know that there are areas that need attention. Equal opportunities, for example, needs more of a positive approach. However we are heading towards certain goals and ideals, not in a hurricane approach, more like a gentle steady progression. Things I wanted to do 12 months ago are now coming to fruition and without a revolution.

The rigorous nature of the process was also evident but practitioners have not been threatened by this. On the contrary, they appear to enjoy the systematic and close examination of their practice and report that this provides them with a greater sense of value and self-worth. A practitioner stated,

I found the whole process a valuable and salutary exercise. I think everyone should confront such probing. It encouraged you to think of how you actually evaluate your practice, how you implement your philosophy and communicate this to others – staff, parents and governors. It highlighted areas where improvement of technique and classroom management are necessary because they have become sloppy or are not actually up and running. It encouraged critical reflection. Do I practise what I preach? Are my values being compromised? Why? How? Do I do this or is this what I would like to achieve? I feel the questions could be used to access any part of the curriculum whatever the emphasis. I'll use them again to evaluate my own practice and I think they could be used as part of in-service work with our own staff or with teachers from other schools in our Early Years Support Group.

An LEA Adviser reported,

The EEL Project has helped me to sharpen up my focus on what I mean by quality in early years provision. I think that the 10 dimensions are a really helpful way of structuring that quality and revealing what it is about. I like the breadth of it. I think it has made us more reflective, and made us look at things in quite a hard-nosed way, which is quite interesting because one of the early criticisms was that it was a soft approach and it is far from this. It is rigorous, it is directed and it is actually making us aware of the choices that we take when putting together a curriculum for the young child.

The process of reflecting, justifying, and rehearsing strengthened the professional understanding of these educators. This honing of their beliefs not only improved the quality of their practice but just as importantly it gave them the tools to become more confident, more knowledgeable and more articulate in their advocacy of the importance of the early years of education.

In Conclusion

Putting in place high quality early learning experiences which are available for all children will not be achieved overnight, and nor will it come cheap. Substantial investment in quality provision for young children is urgently needed and long overdue. We have to be absolutely clear, as limited resources are made available to us, how these might most effectively be used, and what kind of quality provision we are aiming to put in place. The development of rigorous, systematic, manageable and appropriate improvement strategies for early childhood education will be critical in the evolution of policy. The question of quality in early childhood is a crucial one and one which we cannot afford to get wrong.

BIBLIOGRAPHY

Andersson, B. E. (1994) 'Public Policies and Early Childhood Education'. *European Early Childhood Education Research Journal* Volume 2 No. 2: 19–32.

Audit Commission (1996) *Counting to Five, Education of Children under Five. National Report*, London: HMSO.

Aspey, D. N. and Roebuck, F. N. (1977) *Kids don't learn from people they don't like.* Amherst, Massachusetts: Human Resource Development Press.

Ball, Sir C. (1994) *Start Right; The Importance of Early Learning.* London: Royal Society for the Encouragement of Arts, Manufactures & Commerce, RSA.

Bartholomew, L. and Bruce, T. (1993) *Getting to Know You: A Guide to Record-Keeping in Early Childhood Education and Care.* London: Hodder and Stoughton.

Bertram, A. D. (1996) *Effective Educators of Young Children: Developing a Methodology for Improvement.* Doctoral Thesis presented September 1996, Coventry University.

Bredekamp, S. (ed.) (1987) *Developmentally Appropriate Practice in Early Childhood Programs Serving Children Through Age 8.* Washington: National Association for the Education of Young Children.

Brighouse, T. (1995) *Developing Quality in the Early Years.* Presentation to Birmingham Early Years Conference, July 1995 (Unpublished).

British Standards Institute (1991) *Quality Systems: Part 8, Guide to Quality Management and Quality Systems Elements for Services.* London: British Standards Institute.

Brown, A. and Palinscar, A. S. (1989) 'Guided Co-operative Learning and Individual Knowledge' in Resnick, I. B. (ed.) *Knowing Learning Instruction: Essay in Honour of Robert Glaser*, pp. 393–449. Hillsdale, N.J.: Erlbaum.

Brown, A. (1994) 'The Advancement of Learning'. *Educational Researcher*, Volume 23 No. 8: 4–12.

Bruce, T. (1997) (2nd edition) *Early Childhood Education.* London: Hodder and Stoughton.

Bruner, J. S. (1966) *Towards a Theory of Instruction.* Cambridge, Mass.: Harvard University Press.

Bruner, J. S. (1990) *Acts of Meaning*. Cambridge, Mass.: Harvard University Press.

Bruner, J. S. (1966) 'What we have learned about early learning'. *European Early Childhood Education Research Journal*, Volume 4, No. 1: 5–16.

Carnegie Task Force (1994) *Starting Points: Meeting the Needs of Our Young Children*. New York: Carnegie Corporation.

Chapman, M., Skinner, E. A. and Baltes, P. B. (1990) 'Interpreting correlations between children's perceived control and cognitive performance. Control, agency or means-ends beliefs?' *Developmental Psychology*, Volume 23: 246–253.

City of Sheffield Education Department (1992) *Nursery Education*. Sheffield: Sheffield LEA.

Cowley, L. (1991) *Young Children in Group Day Care*. London: National Children's Bureau.

Csikszentmihayli, M. (1992) *Flow: The Psychology of Happiness*. London: Rider.

Curriculum Council for Wales (1991) *Under Fives in School*. Cardiff: Curriculum Council for Wales.

Dahlberg, G. and Åsén, G. (1994) 'Evaluation and Regulation: a Question of Empowerment' in Moss, P. and Pence, A., (eds.) (1994) *Valuing Quality in Early Childhood Services: new approaches to defining quality*. London: Paul Chapman Publishing.

Davies, M. (1995) *Helping Children to Learn Through a Movement Perspective*. London: Hodder and Stoughton.

Department for Education and Employment/Schools Curriculum Assessment Authority (1996) *Desirable Outcomes for Children on Entering Compulsory Schooling*. London: DfEE/SCAA.

Department for Education and Science (1989) *Aspects of Primary Education: The Education of Children Under Five*. London: HMSO.

Department of Education and Science (1990) *Starting with Quality* (the Rumbold Report of the Committee of Inquiry into the Quality of the Educational Experience offered to 3 and 4 year olds). London: HMSO.

Department for Education (1994) *Code of Practice in the Identification and Assessment of Special Educational Needs*. London: HMSO.

Department of Health (1991) *Inspecting for Quality*. London: HMSO.

Devon County Council (1990) *Young Children's Learning: A Curriculum for Three and Four Year Olds*. Exeter: Devon County Council.

Dweck, C. S. and Elliot, E. S. (1979) 'Achievement motivation' in Mussen, P. H. (series ed.) and Hetherington, E. M. (volume ed.), *Handbook of Child Psychology*. (4th Edition). New York: Wiley.

Early Childhood Education and Care Working Group (1988) *Education to be More*. New Zealand Ministry of Education.

EYCG, Early Years Curriculum Group (1989) *Early Childhood Education and the National Curriculum*. Stoke on Trent: Trentham Books.

Edelman, G. M. (1992) *Bright air, brilliant fire; on the matter of the mind*. USA: Basic Books.

Fullan, M. and Hargreaves, A. (1992) *What's Worth Fighting For In Your School?* Milton Keynes: Open University Press.

Goddard, D. and Leask, M. (1992) *The Search for Quality*. London: Paul Chapman Publishers.

Gura, P. (1996) *Resources for Early Learning: Children, Adults and Stuff*. London: Hodder and Stoughton.

Handy, C. (1994) *The Empty Raincoat: Making Sense of the Future*. London: Hutchinson.

Hohmann, M., Banet, B. and Weikart, D. P. (1979) *Young Children in Action: A Manual for Pre-School Educators*. Ypsilanti, Michigan: High/Scope Educational Research Foundation.

Hopkins, D. (1986) *Improving the Quality of Schooling*. London: Falmer Press.

Hopkins, D. (1992) *Evaluation for School Development*. Milton Keynes: Open University Press.

House of Commons (1994) *Educational Provision for the Under Fives*. (Report of the House of Commons Education Committee) London: HMSO.

House of Commons (1996) *Educational Provision for the Under Fives*. (Report of the House of Commons Education Committee) London: HMSO.

Kelly, V. (1994) 'A High Quality Curriculum for the Early Years: Some Conceptual Issues', *Early Years* vol 15, no. 1, p. 6–12.

Kids' Clubs Network (1989) *Guidelines of Good Practice for Out of School Care Schemes*. London: National Out of School Alliance (now KCN).

Laevers, F. (1993) 'Deep Level Learning – An Exemplary Application on the Area of Physical Knowledge'. *European Early Childhood Education Research Journal*, Volume 1, No. 1: 53–68.

Laevers, F. (1994a) *The Leuven Involvement Scale for Young Children LIS-YC*. Manual and Video Tape, Experiential Education Series No. 1, Leuven, Belgium: Centre for Experiential Education.

Laevers, F. (ed.) (1994b) *The Innovative Project 'Experiential Education' and the Definition of Quality in Education*. Leuven: Katholieke Universiteit.

Laevers, F. (1996) (ed.) *An Exploration of the Concept of Involvement as an Indicator for Quality in Early Childhood Education*. Dundee: Scottish Consultative Council on the Curriculum.

Leseman, P., Vergeer, M. M., Sijsling, F. F., Japa-Joe, S. R. and Sahin, S. (1992) *Informal Education in the Home and the Development of Language and Cognition*. Paper presented at the Second European Conference on the Quality of Early Childhood Education, Worcester, UK, 27–29 August.

Louis, F. and Miles, M. B. (1991) *The Empowered School*. London: Cassell.

Matthews, J. (1994) *Helping Children to Draw and Paint in Early Childhood Education*. London: Hodder and Stoughton.

Mooney, A., Munton, T., Rowland, L. and McGurk, H. (1994) *Developing Measures to Assess Quality in Day Care*. Paper presented to Biennial meeting of International Study of Behavioural Development, Amsterdam.

Moss, P. (1994) 'The Early Childhood League in Europe: Problems and Possibilities in Cross-National Comparisons of Levels of Provision'. *European Early Childhood Education Research Journal*, Volume 2, No. 2: 19–32.

Moss, P. and Pence, A., (eds.) (1994) *Valuing Quality in Early Childhood Services: new approaches to defining quality*. London: Paul Chapman Publishing.

Murgatroyd, S. and Morgan, C. (1993) *Total Quality Management and the School*. Milton Keynes: Open University Press.

National Childminding Association (1991) *Setting the Standards*. Bromley: NCMA.

National Commission on Education (1993) *Learning to Succeed; A radical look at education today and a strategy for the future*. (Report of the Paul Hamlyn Foundation National Commission on Education) Oxford: Heinemann.

Office For Standards in Education (OFSTED) (1993 and 1996) *Handbook for the Inspection of Schools*. London: HMSO.

Pascal, C. (1990) *Under Fives in Infant Classrooms*. Trentham Press: Stoke-on-Trent.

Pascal, C. and Bertram, A. D. (1989) 'Diapers in the Department: Don't Be Caught Napping'. *Journal of Modern Management*, Spring 1989.

Pascal, C. and Bertram, A. D. (1994a) 'Evaluating and Improving the Quality of Play' in Moyles, J. (ed.) *The Excellence of Play*. Open University Press: Milton Keynes.

Pascal, C. and Bertram, A. D. (1994b) 'Defining and assessing quality in the education of children from four to seven years' in Laevers, F. (ed.) *Defining and assessing the quality in early childhood education*. Studia Paedagogica, Leuven: Leuven University Press.

Pascal, C., Bertram, A. D. and Heaslip, P. (1989) *ATEE Comparative Directory of Training of Early Years Teachers in Europe*. ATEE: European Commission.

Pascal, C., Bertram, A. D. and Ramsden, F. (1994) *Effective Early Learning: The Quality Evaluation and Development Process*. Worcester: Amber Publications.

Pascal, C., Bertram, A. D., Ramsden, F., Georgeson, J., Saunders, M. and Mould, C. (1995) *Effective Early Learning: Evaluating and Developing Quality in Early Childhood Settings*. Worcester: Amber Publications.

Pascal, C., Bertram, A. D., Ramsden, F., Georgeson, J., Saunders, M. and Mould, C. (1996) *Evaluating and Developing Quality in Early Childhood Settings: A Professional Development Programme*. Worcester: Amber Publications.

Peters, T. (1992) *Liberation Management*. London: Pan MacMillan.

Pfeffer, N. and Coote, A. (1991) *Is Quality Good For You? A Critical Review of Quality Assurance in Welfare Services*. Social Policy Paper No. 5, Institute for Public Policy Research: London.

Piaget, J. (1968) *Six Psychological Studies*. London: University of London Press.

Piaget, J. (1986) *Adaptation and Intelligence*. London: University of Chicago Press, Hermann.

Plaisance, E. (1994) *Pre-school Education and Institutions for Small Children in France: Biological Debates and Facts Concerning Child Minding and Educational Institutions for Children from 0–6 Years of Age*. Paper presented at the 14th

Conference of the Deutsche Gesselschaft für Erziehungwissenschaft, 14–16th March 1994. Dortmund University, Germany.

Pre-School Playgroups Association (now PLA) (1990a) *PPA Guidelines: Good Practice for Sessional Playgroups*. London: PPA.

Pre-School Playgroups Association (now PLA) (1990b) *PPA Guidelines: Good Practice for Full Daycare Playgroups*. London: PPA.

Pre-School Playgroups Association (now PLA) (1993) *Aiming for Quality*. London: PLA.

Pugh, G. (1996) *An Evaluation of the Vouchers Scheme*. Presentation to National Children's Bureau Conference. London: October 1996.

Riley, S. (1984) in Ford, S. (1993) 'The facilitators' role in children's play'. *Young Children* Volume 48, No. 6: 66–69.

Roberts, R. (1995) *Self-Esteem and Successful Early Learning*. London: Hodder and Stoughton.

Rogers, C. (1983) *Freedom to Learn for the 80s*. New York: Macmillan.

Sallis, E. (1993) *Total Quality Management in Education*. London: Kogan Page.

Scheerens, J. (1992) *Effective Schooling: Research, Theory and Practice*. London: Cassell.

Schools' Council (1981) *The Practical Curriculum*. London: Schools' Council.

Schweinhart, L. J. and Weikart, D. P. (1993) *A Summary of Significant Benefits: The High/Scope Perry Pre-school Study Through Age 27*. Ypsilanti, Michigan: High/Scope Press.

Skinner, E. A. and Belmont, M. J. (1993) 'Motivation in the Classroom: reciprocal effects of teacher behaviour and student engagement across the school year'. *Journal of Educational Psychology*, Volume 85, No. 4: 571–581.

Smiley, P. A. and Dweck, C. (1994) Individual Differences in Achievement Goals among Young Children. *Child Development*, Volume 65: 1723–1743.

Sylva, K., Roy, C. and Painter, M. (1980) *Childwatching at Playgroup and Nursery School*. Oxford Preschool Research Project. London: Grant-McIntyre.

Sylva, K. and Wiltshire, J. (1993) 'The Impact of Early Learning on Children's Later Development'. *European Early Childhood Education Research Journal*, Volume 1, No. 1: 17–40.

Times Educational Supplement (1995) *Diversity and Mess*. 27th January 1995.

Trevarthen, C. (1995) *'How Children Learn Before School'*, text of a lecture to BAECE, Newcastle University, 2 November 1993.

Vygotsky, L. S. (1978) *Mind in Society*. Cambridge, Mass.: Harvard University Press.

West-Burnham, J. (1992) *Managing Quality in Schools*. London: Longman.

Whalley, M. (1994) *Learning to be Strong: Integrating Education and Care in Early Childhood*. London: Hodder and Stoughton.

Whitehead, M. (1996) *The Development of Language and Literacy*. London: Hodder and Stoughton.

Wilkinson, E. and Stephen, C. (1992) *Evaluating Ourselves*. University of Glasgow.

Williams, P. (1995) *Making Sense of Quality: A Review of Approaches to Quality in Early Childhood Services*. London: National Children's Bureau.

Young, M. E. (1995) *Investing in Young Children*. World Bank Discussion Papers 275, The World Bank, Washington, DC.

INDEX

Accreditation 15
Action initiatives 16–17
Action Planning 11, 13, 14, 20, 26–27, 45–47, 59–61, 77–78, 91–93, 105–106, 119–121, 135–136, 145–146, 155
Aims and Objectives 8, 67, 102, 118
Assertiveness 34, 36, 41
Autonomy 13, 17, 23, 58, 77–82, 91, 120–121, 124–125, 126, 133, 144, 147–148

Behaviour Management 92–94, 107–108

Children Act 1989 72
Csikszentmihayli 6

Democratic Approach 10, 151–152

Early Literacy 26–30
EEL Project:
    Aims 3
    Development 4
    Dimensions of Quality 7–9
    Evaluative Framework 7–9, 152–153
    External Validation 3, 14, 151
    Support Worker 20, 45, 46, 49, 51, 55, 60, 65, 72–74, 87–88, 101, 117, 124, 130, 140
    Values and Principles 9–10
Empowerment 155
Engagement 11, 12–13, 64, 76, 81, 88, 91, 95, 102, 104, 109, 124, 130, 135, 148, 154
Equal Opportunities 9, 25, 31, 34, 61
Evaluation 11, 20–25, 44–45, 55, 56–59, 74–77, 88–91, 102–104, 130, 143–145, 150
Evaluation Report 13, 20, 25, 74, 91, 120, 131, 145

Family Centre 32–51
Family Worker 33, 37, 40–42, 44, 46, 49
Father 33, 34, 36, 37, 69
Final Report 20
Funding 66, 81

Gender 23, 25, 34
Group time 48 49, 50

Headteacher 109, 143, 146–147
Health Visitor 32, 34
Home Visits 84, 92–93

Improvement 11, 14, 17, 27–28, 47–49, 78–81, 106–108, 122–124
Inspection 15, 151–152
Interviews 55, 101, 131
Involvement 6, 11–12, 22–23, 29–30, 45, 46, 50, 57, 58, 61, 63, 73, 75, 79, 81–82, 88, 90–91, 94, 103–104, 117, 119, 122, 126, 130, 135, 144–145, 154

Key Worker 61–62, 64, 84–85, 90

Laevers 6
LEA Nursery Class 95–110

LEA Nursery School 18–31
Learning Experiences/Curriculum 8, 24, 44, 57, 58, 60, 61, 78, 89–90, 99, 103, 108–109, 118, 121, 131–132, 141–143, 146, 147–148
Learning and Teaching Strategies 8, 75, 118

Management, Monitoring and Evaluation 9, 40, 47, 142
Management Committee 55, 56, 57, 60–63, 66, 73
Mastery 7

Observation 22, 24, 31, 40, 51, 58, 74, 76, 79, 81, 88, 101–102, 117, 120, 122, 131–132, 152
Outcomes 153–154

Parental Partnership 9, 24, 25, 26, 30, 35–37, 40, 41, 42, 51, 57, 61–63, 66, 72, 77, 83, 92–93, 101–102, 108, 119, 125, 135–136, 146–147
Photographs 131
Physical Environment 8, 34–35, 52–53, 58, 67–71, 85–87, 98–99, 105, 112–115, 125, 128–129, 138–139
Piaget 5
Planning, Assessment and Record Keeping 8, 24, 42, 45, 46, 47–48, 50, 61, 94
Play 37, 57, 61, 67, 68, 73, 75, 79, 103–106, 108, 110, 132, 145–146
Policy 84
Pre-school Playgroup 66–82
Private Day Nursery 52–65, 111–127
Process 153–154

Quality 7

Reception Class 138–149
Reflection 11, 14, 28–31, 49–50, 63 65, 81–82, 95–97, 108–110, 125–127, 136–137, 147–149, 157–158
Relationships and interactions 9, 76, 92, 118, 134
Routines and Organisation 54–55, 60, 61, 64, 83–84, 88–89, 99–100, 105, 110–112, 129, 139
Rumbold Report 131

Sensitivity 13, 23, 76, 81, 91
Social Services Day Nursery 83–97
Special Educational Needs 39, 83–84, 96
Staffing 8, 31, 35–36, 53–54, 71–72, 84–85, 99, 116, 139
Staff Development 50–51, 60, 68, 79, 82, 92–94, 107, 154–155
State of Flow 6
Stimulation 13, 23, 30, 58, 76, 81
Strategies for Improvement 3

Teamwork 27, 51
Timescale 14–15, 153, 156
TV 86, 89, 91

Vygotsky 5

Working Together 20, 55–56, 72–74, 87–88, 101–102, 117–119, 130, 140–143
Work Place Nursery 128–137

Zones of Development 5